Longman exam practice kit

GCSE Information Technology

Roger Crawford

LONGMAN

Series Editors
Geoff Black and Stuart Wall

Titles available

GCSE	*A-level*
Biology	Biology
Business Studies	British and European Modern History
Chemistry	Business Studies
English	Chemistry
French	Economics
German	French
Geography	German
Higher Mathematics	Geography
Information Systems	Mathematics
Mathematics	Physics
Physics	Psychology
Science	Sociology

Addison Wesley Longman Ltd,
Edinburgh Gate, Harlow, Essex
CM20 2JE, England
and Associated Companies throughout the World

First published 1998

ISBN 0582 31249-3

British Library Cataloguing-in-Publication Data
A catalogue record for this book is available from the British Library.

Set by 30 in 11/13pt Baskerville

Produced by Longman Singapore Publishers Pte
Printed in Singapore

Contents

Author's preface

Throughout this book the emphasis is on preparation for the written examinations in GCSE Information Technology (IT). The practice exercises are grouped into coherent topic areas that will be immediately recognizable to teachers with experience of delivering the IT National Curriculum programmes of study, or preparing candidates for GCSE assessment. The topic areas are arranged in a logical order but it is not necessary for students to work through them in the order they appear. Each topic area is self-contained and can be used independently. It is likely that many of the practice exercises will also be useful in developing students' knowledge and understanding as they acquire the skills they need to do their GCSE IT coursework projects. In addition, there are timed practice papers that include questions from a variety of topic areas. Students may find these useful as they approach the written examinations at the end of their course of study.

In writing this book I have valued the help and advice given to me both directly and indirectly. My thanks go to editorial staff at Longman, especially Bridget Allen, and to Stuart Wall and Geoff Black of Guidelines Publishing. I am grateful to colleagues at Rhodesway Upper School, Bradford and at Queensbury School, Bradford for their help and inspiration while I was employed at each school. I am particularly grateful for the assistance given to me by the School of Education at the University of Huddersfield where I am now employed as a Senior Lecturer in Education specializing in IT. My wife, Jennie, has patiently tolerated the long hours I have spent at the wordprocessor. Without the support of colleagues, friends and family this book would not have been written.

Roger Crawford

Acknowledgements
The following institutions, and commercial and industrial companies have kindly given their permission to use material for illustration or to refer to their products.

Barclays Bank Plc
Camelot Group Plc
Lloyds TSB Group Plc
Microsoft Corporation
The University of Huddersfield

The following GCSE examination boards have given permission, where appropriate, for questions from their specimen or examination papers to be used. The answers or hints on answers have been written by the author and have not been provided or approved by any examination board. The questions may not indicate the format and content of future examination papers.

London (now known as the Edexcel Foundation)	RSA
MEG	SEG
NDTEF	WJEC
NEAB	

How to use this book

This book covers the main topics in GCSE Information Technology, and is aimed at helping you achieve a good grade in your examination. The book is split into four parts.

Part I Preparing for the examination

This section covers what you should be doing before and during the examination. It will help you to plan your revision, remind you of the things that you should be doing before and on the actual day, and help you to understand what is required by the actual questions by looking at key words. A revision planner is provided at the end of this book to help you structure your revision, beginning some weeks before the examination.

Part II The topic areas

This section has been divided into seven common topic areas. In each topic chapter you will find the following:

1 **Revision tips** These give useful summary information about the topic and revision hints to help you learn the topic more easily.
2 **Topic outline** These will not replace your own full notes but will give most of the basic facts that you need and give you material in short fact form that is easier to revise. Make sure that you can expand more fully on the key facts identified in the topic area.
3 **Revision activities** These exercises are aimed at making your revision active. They will help you to self-check your understanding of that topic area. Try these activities after you have revised the topic, before you attempt the practice questions. Answers are found in Part III.
4 **Practice questions** These questions are very similar to the type of question you are likely to face in the examination. Do try hard to answer the questions to the best of your ability before you look up the answers in Part III. Don't give up too easily or you aren't making the best use of the questions.

Part III All the answers

Here you will find suggested answers to revision activities and practice questions.

Part IV Timed practice papers

This section provides two practice papers, one at Foundation Level and one at Higher Level, to attempt under exam-like conditions. Check your progress by marking the paper using the answers and marking schemes provided.

part I

Preparing for the examination

Revision and exam techniques

Why is achieving a good grade in GCSE Information Technology (IT) important to you? If you know why you need a good grade you may work harder and do better. Students often find IT interesting and enjoyable, and it may be a useful preparation for work. Many jobs in IT are well paid! Convince yourself it is important to succeed. Always do your best work. If you have a clear idea of why you are studying IT you may find it easier to put in the effort required to do well. If you are well motivated you are already on the road to success. However, to do well in an exam you also need to pay careful attention to preparing yourself for it.

The purpose of an exam is to test your knowledge and understanding. If you do not know your subject then you cannot expect to do well. Preparation for the exam begins on the first day of the course.

▶ Try not to miss lessons. If you do, catch up with the work quickly.
▶ Keep all the notes you write and the work you do.
▶ Do all your homework to your best standard.
▶ Learn your work as you progress. If you have any spare time, go back over the course and revise the work. Make sure you understand all the work you do.
▶ Use the library to look up topics you are unsure of.
▶ If you have problems, ask your teacher.

You can enrich your knowledge and understanding in a variety of ways.

▶ Read computer magazines.
▶ Go to local shops that sell computers and ask the sales staff about the computers they sell.
▶ Go on trips to computer exhibitions.
▶ Talk to someone who works with IT systems and ask them about their job.
▶ Arrange a visit to an office or factory where IT systems are used.
▶ Get your own computer and learn to use it.

Start revising in good time and plan your revision carefully. You can use the revision planner at the end of this book. Try to allocate set times each week when you will revise for your GCSE IT exam. Make sure you allow time to revise all the subjects you are taking, and build in periods for rest and relaxation. Expect to work very hard in the weeks leading up to your GCSE exams but leave some time to enjoy yourself. Overwork and worry can be as bad as not doing anything.

When you are revising for an exam this is the time to make sure you have learnt all you need to know. Be clear about what you have to learn. Make a list of all the topics you should cover.

A useful revision technique is to **repeatedly revise**, **condense** and **learn**. Read through your notes and all the work you have done and, as you revise your knowledge, take a brief note of all the topics. These brief notes should cover all the important points in enough detail to refresh your memory of them at a later date. Try and learn these brief notes. If there is still too much material to learn, then condense these brief notes yet again. You should end up with condensed notes which summarize the whole course. These can be learnt and revised frequently. You can carry them with you and revise on the bus, in the queue for the cinema, or taking the dog for a walk!

Practise for the exam by doing questions of the kind you will meet in exams. There are plenty of these in this book! Work through them carefully. Check your answers and, if you have made a mistake, make sure that you understand why you have made it. It is likely that similar questions will appear on the exam papers you will take.

Nearer to the exam try to complete the practice papers under exam conditions in the time allowed for them. This will give you some idea of how fast you will have to work in the exam. If you find you are short of time, plan ahead and use your time effectively.

USING EXAMINATION QUESTIONS IN REVISION

▶ After you have thoroughly revised a topic, you need to check that you have understood the topic.

▶ Do some questions similar to those you will find in the exam. You will find some in this book. This could reveal your strengths and weaknesses.

▶ Revise those topics where you have weaknesses again. You can make extra notes on them if you need to. Do more practice questions in these topic areas until you are confident you understand what is required.

▶ You could identify those topics you understand, and answer questions on these in the exam. Perhaps you will be able to avoid questions on topics you are not so familiar with.

▶ You will become more familiar with the language used in exam questions. You might find it useful to refer to the list of command words given later in this section.

▶ You can find out what examiners are looking for when they mark your work by checking your answers against the answers given in Part III. The 'student answers with examiner comments' will show you how examiners view students' answers.

▶ Nearer to the exam you should practice answering questions under exam conditions. In Part IV you will find practice exam papers that you may find useful.

Types of examination question

Questions on exam papers in IT usually have space for you to answer on the paper. They are often quite short. Longer questions are usually carefully structured and lead you step-by-step through the question. You may encounter some essay-type questions but these will rarely ask you to write at length.

It is important to notice how much space has been provided for you to write your answer in. This indicates the length of answer the examiner expects. Provided your answer is relevant and focused, you should be able to answer the question in the space provided. If you leave space, you probably have not done enough; if you need much more space, then you have probably missed the point of the question or are giving too much detail.

You may come across these types of question:

▶ **Fill in** questions expect you to fill in a word in a sentence. The sentence will be printed with a word missing and a space will be left for you to write in the correct word. Sometimes you will be given a list of words to choose from. If the question asks you to fill in a word, fill in one word and make sure it is clear which word you have filled in.

▶ **Multiple choice** questions give you a series of alternatives to choose from. You will be asked to show which choice you think is correct by ticking a box, or ringing a word or phrase. If you are asked to tick two boxes, only tick two boxes. Ticking more than two boxes will not help you gain marks as examiners will deduct marks if there are extra ticks.

▶ **Short answer** questions expect you to give a brief answer. You may have to name a piece of hardware, or state an advantage or disadvantage.

▶ **Extended answer** questions require you to write a short essay. As with an essay, you will have to decide how you are going to structure your answer and what aspects of the topic you are going to emphasize.

▶ **Design** questions expect you to complete a given design or produce a whole design. You will be required to draw part or all of a diagram. You may be asked to label the diagram in some way. For example, you could be asked to draw a line on a flowchart that is given to you, draw a diagram of a computer network, or design a questionnaire.

Command words used in questions

What follows is a list of the words that tell you what to do when you answer an exam question. As with all language, these words are often slightly ambiguous and are sometimes only different ways of saying almost the same thing. When you are deciding what to do, you should always refer to the way the question is presented.

▶ **Tick** You are expected to place a tick in a box to indicate your chosen answer.

▶ **Ring** You are expected to draw a ring round your chosen answer.

▶ **Fill in** You are expected to write in a word or phrase in the space provided.

▶ **Complete** You are expected to finish off a sentence, or a short program, part of which is given in the exam paper.

▶ **Name** You are expected to write down the name of some process or artefact. For example, a piece of hardware.

▶ **State** You are expected to write a short answer, probably a single word, phrase or sentence.

▶ **Suggest** You are expected to write a short answer, probably a single word, phrase or sentence.

▶ **Write down** You are expected to write a short answer, probably a single word, phrase or sentence.

▶ **Give** You are expected to write a short answer, probably a single word, phrase or sentence.

▶ **List** You are expected to give a series of short answers to the same question.

▶ **Describe** You are expected to write a short account of what is done or observed. For example, how a cashpoint is used.

▶ **Describe in detail** You are expected to write a fuller description that gives particular attention to what you are describing.

▶ **Explain** You are expected to write an account of how something works or why something is done.

▶ **Compare and contrast** You are expected to write about the similarities and differences between two or more processes or artefacts.

▶ **In this context** In your answer, you should pay particular attention to the situation described in the question and refer to it.

▶ **Label** You are expected to name the different parts of a diagram on the diagram.

▶ **Modify** You are expected to make changes on a diagram given to you.

▶ **Draw** You are expected to modify a diagram given to you, or sketch a whole diagram and label it.

▶ **Design** You are expected to sketch a whole diagram, label it if necessary, and possibly write an accompanying description or explanation of your design.

Assessment objectives in Information Technology

Assessment objectives vary between syllabuses. However, they are all very similar. Typically, the coursework and exams will test your ability to:

1 Apply your knowledge, skills and understanding of IT in a variety of circumstances.
2 Analyse, design, implement, test, evaluate, and document IT systems for your own use and for others to use.

3 Develop an understanding of the wider applications of IT.

4 Reflect critically on the way you and others use IT.

5 Discuss and review the impact of using IT systems.

6 Consider the social, legal, ethical and moral issues, and the need for security when IT is used.

Coursework assessment is likely to concentrate on assessment objective 2, while the exams will, on the whole, cover the remaining objectives.

During the examination

However much you know, you will perform better if you are wide awake, healthy and relaxed. Look after yourself! You are likely to do your best work if you are alert. Alertness depends on good health, plenty of sleep and a calm determination to do well.

► Make sure you go to the lavatory just before the exam. You could waste five or ten minutes of valuable exam time if you have to go during the exam!

► Make sure you get plenty of sleep in the days before the exam. Go to bed reasonably early and you will be more alert and cope with the exam much better.

► You are also likely to perform better if you are fit and healthy. A bad cold, hay fever, headaches, broken bones, sprained ankles and other maladies can distract you from your work in the exam. The best remedy is to avoid accidents and situations that could make you ill. The day before your exam may not be the right time to go horse riding, skiing, sky diving, etc. If you have unavoidable medical problems, your doctor may be able to help.

► Many people find that exams make them nervous. They get so nervous they make silly mistakes and are unable to do their best. Most people are affected by exam nerves to some extent. Being too nervous will probably have a bad effect on your work. On the other hand, some people are so relaxed they do sloppy, careless work. Being too relaxed is as inappropriate as being too nervous. Make sure you are keen to do well but keep calm.

Exam techniques are not magic! Using exam techniques will not make up for lack of thorough preparation or ignorance. Exam techniques are common sense methods to help you communicate what you know more effectively.

► Before you arrive at the exam, make sure you have any equipment you will need in the exam. You will require a pencil, a pencil sharpener, a rubber, a ruler and at least two pens, in case one runs out. A calculator might be useful. This equipment is essential for accurate, written communication. If you have to borrow a pen, for example, it may not suit you or it may not work properly and consequently you may work at a slower pace. It is possible that equipment may not be available to borrow and you will have to manage without it.

► Always arrive on time for an exam. If you are late you will not be allowed extra time.

► Start work as soon as you are allowed to.

► Read the instructions at the start of the exam very carefully, and do what you are asked.

► The first task in any exam is to make sure you know which questions you are expected to answer. Doing extra questions will not earn extra marks but if you leave questions out you will lose marks.

► Next, work out how much time you can spend on each question. It is often useful to work out how much time you can devote to each mark. This is the number of minutes per mark. You can use this to work out how long can be spent on questions that may not be worth the same amount of marks. For example, in a one hour paper you may have 60 minutes to earn perhaps 60 marks. This is 1 minute per mark. This means that you can spend 2 minutes on a question worth 2 marks, and 6 minutes on a question worth 6 marks, and so on. Having worked out the time you can spend on a question, stick to it.

► Attempt all the questions you are expected to answer. This is very important. The first part of each question is often the easiest to answer and the first few marks on any question are often the easiest to obtain. You cannot be given marks for questions you haven't answered. Higher marks will almost certainly be given for correct answers to part of all the required questions than for complete answers to a very few questions.

► Make sure you read the question thoroughly. Many students lose marks because they read the question in a hurry and do not fully grasp what it means. They then answer the question they think they have read. This means their answer may not relate to the actual question. You will only be awarded marks for a correct answer to the actual question set. **Read questions slowly and carefully**.

► If it is difficult to read your answers, you will probably lose marks. Write neatly and set out your work clearly.

► If necessary, give examples and draw diagrams to illustrate your answers. Communicate clearly and in full.

► You will be given extra marks for good spelling, punctuation and grammar.

► Never leave an exam before the end. Spend all the time allowed to you to do the exam answering questions or checking your answers. Make sure that what you can do is correct and make a determined attempt at the more difficult questions. Marks are always given for correct answers but it is not often that marks are deducted if you are wrong.

Communicating information

Remember the different ways to **generate text**:

▶ you can input it using a keyboard;
▶ you can scan it from a book using OCR software;
▶ you can export it from one piece of software and import it into another, for example, you can export text written in a wordprocessor and import it into DTP software;
▶ you can copy it from CD-ROM or the WWW and paste it into a document;
▶ you can download it using e-mail.

Remember the different ways to **generate graphics**:

▶ you can scan line drawings or photographs using a flatbed scanner;
▶ you can take a photograph using a digital camera and download it;
▶ you can copy an image from a clip art library;
▶ you can produce a line drawing using a graphics pad;
▶ you can grab a frame from a video.

Do not just remember *facts*. If possible, make sure you can use:

▶ a wordprocessor;   ▶ multimedia;
▶ graphics software;   ▶ e-mail;
▶ DTP;   ▶ video conferencing.

Make sure you can:

▶ load (or open) a document;   ▶ enter and edit text, and change its font, style and size;
▶ save (or close) a document;   ▶ import, export and edit graphics;
▶ print;   ▶ copy, cut and paste text and graphics.

TOPIC OUTLINE

Why and to whom information is communicated

▶ All information is communicated for a purpose, to an audience.
  – The **audience** is the group of people that a communication is directed at.
  – The **purpose** is the reason the communication takes place.
  For example, a salesperson could communicate with an audience of potential customers with the purpose of selling them goods.
▶ The audience may not always be the same. For example, at a different time, the salesperson could communicate with his/her employer.
▶ Even if the audience is the same, the purpose may change. For example, the salesperson could communicate with his/her employer in the hope of being awarded an increase in pay, or regarding the poor quality of some goods that he/she has to sell.
▶ A change in purpose may change the **emphasis** in presenting the content of a communication. For example, when asking his/her employer for a pay increase the salesperson may suggest that the high volume of sales of a product is due to

the excellent personal service he/she gives to customers, but when explaining why customers are dissatisfied the salesperson may focus on the lack of attention given to some aspect of manufacturing.

▶ The extent to which the audience is likely to **understand** what is being communicated should be taken into account. When communicating information, try to be clear, simple and interesting, and present information in a straightforward and logical way. Be sure that the audience is capable of understanding what is being communicated. Get the level right. If the content is too easy, the audience will be bored; if it is too complex, the audience will not understand.

▶ Make sure the information is **relevant**. Include enough information but not too much or too little. If there is too much information that diverges too widely from the focus of the communication then the audience will probably be confused. If there is too little information, its relevance may not be obvious.

Software

Software for wordprocessing, graphics, desk top publishing (DTP), e-mail, multimedia and video conferencing is particularly useful for **communicating information** although to some extent all IT tools can be used for this. Each type of software has overlapping capabilities and functions but each has distinctive features. Some of these are described below:

Wordprocessor

Using a **wordprocessor** (see Figure 1.1), you can:

▶ write a letter, a leaflet, an essay, a c.v., a questionnaire, etc.;
▶ create, save, open or load, and print wordprocessing documents;
▶ move around a document by scrolling up and down it, and scrolling sideways;
▶ insert, delete and edit text;
▶ use different text fonts and sizes, and generate word art;
▶ move, cut, copy and paste blocks of text and graphics;

Figure 1.1
Using a
wordprocessor

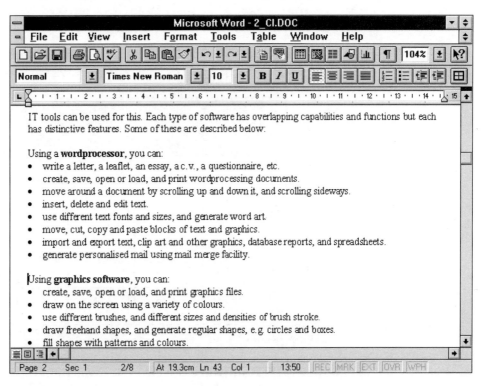

▶ import and export text, clip art and other graphics, database reports, and spreadsheets;
▶ generate personalized mail using mail merge facility.

Graphics software

Using **graphics software** (see Figure 1.2), you can:

► create, save, open or load, and print graphics files;
► draw on the screen using a variety of colours;
► use different brushes, and different sizes and densities of brush stroke;
► draw freehand shapes, and generate regular shapes, e.g. circles and boxes;
► fill shapes with patterns and colours;
► use different text fonts and sizes;
► zoom in and out to edit text and graphics;
► move, cut, copy and paste blocks of text and graphics;
► import and export scanned images, video frames, clip art and other graphics.

Figure 1.2
Using graphics
software

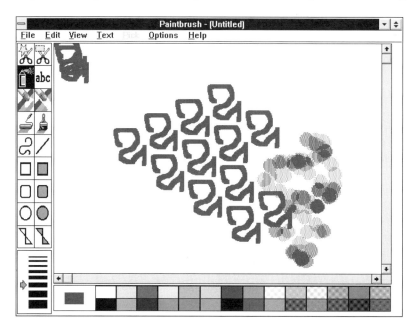

Desk top publishing (DTP)

Figure 1.3
Using DTP
software

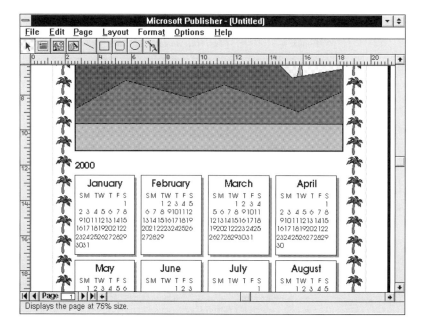

Using **DTP software** (see Figure 1.3), you can:

► lay out the pages of a newsletter, magazine, etc. with some precision;
► create, save, open or load, and print DTP pages;
► import and export text, scanned images, video frames, clip art and other graphics, database reports, and spreadsheets;

- view the page in different magnifications, zoom in and out;
- move around a page by scrolling up and down it, and scrolling sideways;
- move, cut, copy and paste blocks of text and graphics to arrange information on a page;
- use different text fonts and sizes, and generate word art.

Multimedia
Using **multimedia** software, you can:

- view multimedia encyclopaedias, etc. that combine graphics, text, video and sound, and navigation aids, probably stored on CD-ROM;
- produce multimedia presentations.

Electronic mail (e-mail)
Using **e-mail**, you can:

- send and receive messages, nationally and internationally, using the Internet;
- set up address books and mailing lists;
- save messages and print them.

Video conferencing
Using **video conferencing**, you can:

- see the people you are talking to on the screen and hear what they are saying;
- share screens for graphics or other applications so that you can discuss what you are doing with them or develop your work collaboratively at a distance;
- take part in a continuing debate on subjects that interest you with people who live in different places.

REVISION ACTIVITIES

Question 1
Tick **three** boxes to show which of the following statements are true.

	Tick three boxes
You can load and save files using a wordprocessing, DTP and graphics software.	
IT makes it harder for people to communicate.	
There is very little that you cannot do with a modern PC.	
You can communicate very quickly over long distances using e-mail.	
Using video conferencing, you can see and talk to people in other countries.	
You should make everything very complicated so nobody understands you.	

Question 2
Ring the features you would expect to find in graphics software.

brush size adjustment	audience participation	enlargement
mail merge	colour palette	formulae
freehand drawing tool	zoom in and out	key fields
e-mail	block copy, cut and paste	box drawing tool

Question 3

(a) Using words from the list, complete the sentences:

font   line   calculation   paragraph   size

- In a wordprocessor, you press the <ENTER> key to start a new ....
- Times New Roman is the name of a popular ....

(b) Using words from the list, write down the style of text used.

strikethrough   bold   italics   capitals   bullets   underline

	Style of text used
style of text	
style of text	
<u>style of text</u>	
~~style of text~~	
STYLE OF TEXT	

Question 4

(a) Ring the facilities you would expect to find in DTP software.

load or open a file	video editing	fax
set up a key field	use a different font	print
import clip art	save or close a file	use a different text size
sound recording	re-size clip art	create relationships

(b) A secretary is using DTP software to publish a newsletter.
Tick **three** boxes to show the tasks the secretary might do using the DTP software.

	Tick three boxes
Layout text and graphics in columns.	
Send e-mail.	
Edit an article that has been imported from a wordprocessor.	
Import a picture taken using a digital camera.	
Edit sound and music.	
Scan a photograph into the computer.	

Question 5

(a) Using words from the list complete the sentences.

student   security alarm company   doctor   textile designer   teacher

- A .... could use DTP to produce more attractive worksheets.
- A .... could use video conferencing to treat an injured worker on an oil rig.
- A .... could use e-mail to send messages to its maintenance engineers.
- A .... could use a multimedia encyclopaedia to look up information.
- A .... could use graphics software to try out new patterns.

(b) Give three advantages to a school pupil in using IT to communicate information.

PRACTICE QUESTIONS

Question 1

(a) Tick **three** boxes to show which of the following statements are true.

	Tick three boxes
You do not need to have a network connection to send e-mail.	
Different text styles and fonts can be used in a wordprocessing document.	
Video conferencing is not likely to be used very much because it is much more enjoyable to meet your friends and have a relaxed chat.	
Wordprocessors are less flexible than manual typewriters	
You can make several printed copies of a document prepared using a wordprocessor.	
If you do not save your work, when you switch off the computer it will be lost.	

(b) Using words from the list, complete the sentences.

DTP   e-mail   graphics software   multimedia   spreadsheets   video conferencing   wordprocessing

(i) .... can be used to arrange text and graphics on a page in columns as in a newspaper.

(ii) .... can be used to send electronic messages.

(iii) .... can be used to write letters and other documents.

Question 2

(a) Name a wordprocessor you have used.
(b) Describe the hardware the wordprocessor runs on.
(c) Describe how you would use the wordprocessor to:
(i) Load or open a document.   (iv) Check your spelling.
(ii) Use different text sizes.   (v) Print a document.
(iii) Move a block of text.   (vi) Save or close a document.

Question 3

(a) A science teacher is using DTP software to write a worksheet. Describe how a diagram could be moved from one part of the worksheet to another.
(b) Explain why the science teacher may wish to see the worksheet displayed on the screen in different magnifications.
(c) What type of printer would be best for printing the worksheet? Give a reason for your answer.

Question 4

QUICKMIX make food processors.

(a) A secretary is writing a letter to a customer. State the hardware and software needed to do this.
(b) The secretary wants to include a picture of a food processor in the letter. Describe the additional hardware and software needed, and explain how this could be done.

(c) The secretary wants to send a personalized letter to all customers using mail merge. Explain what is meant by mail merge, and describe how it is done.

Question 5
An engineer services security alarms throughout Scotland. The engineer works for a company based in Burnley. The company employs several other engineers who also cover large areas of the country.

(a) Describe how e-mail could be used improve communications between the company and its engineers.
(b) Draw a diagram showing the hardware needed to communicate using e-mail.
(c) Describe how an e-mail message is sent.
(d) State one advantage and one disadvantage to the company of using e-mail.
(e) An engineer is sent to Pakistan to install a security alarm system for contractors working on the construction of a hydroelectric dam. Discuss the advantages and disadvantages of e-mail to the engineer.

Question 6
The Blackbird clothes shop has branches in Crouch End, Oswaldtwistle and Settle. It is having a sale. In all its branches, the price of jeans has been reduced by 10 per cent until the end of the week, and socks are down from £5 to £3 for 4 pairs.

(a) Design a poster advertising the sale.
(b) Name the software you would use to produce the poster.
(c) Describe four features of the software that make it suitable for producing the poster.
(d) State four items of information that should be in the poster.
(e) Describe four ways of importing an image of a blackbird so that it can be included in the poster.

Question 7
Give one advantage and one disadvantage of video conferencing to:

(a) A student who wants to learn to speak Japanese.
(b) An oil rig worker who has been injured and needs medical treatment.
(c) Young people who live in remote regions of Scotland where there are no local schools.

Question 8
Describe two ways each of the following could make use of IT to communicate information so that they can do their jobs more effectively.

(a) A journalist.
(b) A graphic designer.
(c) A town planner.

Question 9
The Silsden Tennis Club is having a dance to raise funds.

(a) The Secretary uses desk top publishing (DTP) software to design a poster to advertise the dance.

Complete the sentences using terms from the list.

   clip art   columns   fonts   pixels   sizes

   – DTP software helps the Secretary lay out text and graphics in .... on the poster.

   – The Secretary can import .... into the DTP software.   [2]

(b) The Secretary prints the poster on a laser printer.
Tick **one** box to show why a laser printer is used.   [1]

	Tick one box
A laser printer costs less to buy than a dot matrix printer.	
A laser printer costs less to run than a dot matrix printer.	
A laser printer is environmentally friendly.	
A laser printer prints good quality text and graphics.	
A laser printer prints good quality text but cannot print graphics.	

(c) Some Tennis Club members believe that the Secretary should not use
Information Technology. Give a reasoned argument why the Tennis Club should
not use Information Technology.   [4]
SEG

Question 10

The local council is going to organize a summer fete. The chairman of the council
has suggested that a computer be used to help in the organization, planning and
running of the fete. One of the members of the local council has used desk top
publishing software to produce the following poster to advertise the fete.

Figure 1.4

The desk top publishing package used has several features available in its menus.

(a) Describe **two** features of the desk top publishing package used to produce different
parts of the poster.   [4]
(b) In addition to wordprocessing and desk top publishing software the council
member wishes to use other software to help with the fete.
Name **two** other **different** types of software which could be used in the
organization, administration or running of the fete.   [2]
(c) For **one** of the pieces of software you have given describe what data are needed
and what the data will be used for.   [2]
WJEC

Handling information and databases

Remember:

► what is meant by a **database**, a **file**, a **record**, and a **field**;
► that a field can contain alphanumeric and numeric data, and dates and times;
► that each record should have a unique key field that identifies it;
► that a field can be coded and why it is coded.

Remember the different ways to collect information, using:

► a questionnaire;
► OMR;
► OCR;

► bar codes;
► magnetic stripe cards.

Remember that the information collected should be checked, and that:

► verification checks that data captured is accurately input, using the double entry method;
► validation checks that the data captured is reasonable, using length checks, type checks, table look-ups, range checks and check digits.

Do not just remember facts. If possible, make sure you can access information stored on:

► a database;
► CD-ROM;
► an on-line library catalogue;

► teletext;
► the World Wide Web.

Make sure you can:

► load and save a database;
► edit, insert and delete database records and fields;
► search, sort, select and print information;
► backup a file and restore it.

You need to know about information handling, particularly how databases, teletext and the World Wide Web handle information. These are some of the key points:

Databases

A **database** (see Figure 2.1) is an organized collection of information consisting of one or more files (or tables).

Files, records, fields

► A database **file** (or table) is a collection of related records. For example, a file of information about all the pupils in a school.
► A **record** in a database file is a collection of related fields. In records of the same type, the fields are in the same order. For example, each teacher's record might include their teacher number, family name, first name, and form in the same order.

Figure 2.1
Using a database

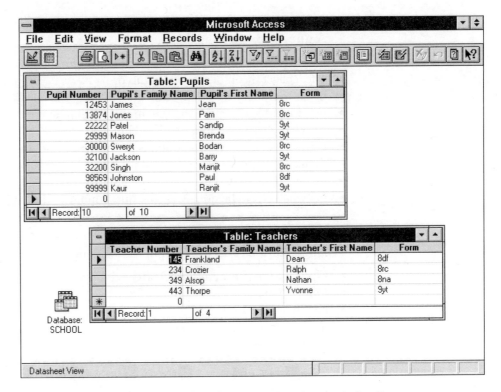

▸ A **field** is an item of information. For example, a teacher's family name.

▸ A **fieldname** is the name given to a field. For example, the field containing a teacher number might have the fieldname TEA_NUM.

▸ A **key field** uniquely identifies a record. For example, each teacher will have a teacher number that identifies the teacher and their record in the database. No two teachers will have the same teacher number. In this case, the teacher number could be used as the key field.

▸ Fields can have different **data types**. That is, they can contain different types of data. Some common examples are:
  – **alphanumeric** (0 to 9; A to Z; and symbols such as £);
  – **numeric**, that is: *integer* (positive and negative whole numbers, e.g. 45, –89) or *real* (any number, e.g. –23.45, 6.342);
  – **date** (a date in a standard format, e.g. YYMMDD, that is, 970612 would mean the 12th of June 1997);
  – **time** (the time in a standard format, e.g. 13.34 hours).

▸ Fields may be coded. **Codes** should be short yet meaningful. For example, the way in which a customer pays could be coded like this:

way a customer pays	code
cash	ca
credit card, e.g. visa	cr
cheque	ch
debit card	de
store card	st

Fields are coded to save time when entering data and to reduce the storage space required when information is saved on backing storage.

Data collection

Data collection can be done using a questionnaire or other form, or using methods of direct data capture and input.

Questionnaires

A **questionnaire** should:

► have a title and introduction explaining its purpose;
► only collect the information required;
► be clear and precise about what information is needed;
► provide sufficient space to write in the information;
► use character boxes to assist data entry;
► use tick lists to show what options are available and assist data entry;
► thank the respondent for filling it in;
► be signed and dated by the respondent;
► say what should be done with the questionnaire when it has been filled in.

Direct data capture

Direct **data capture** and input can be done using:

► Optical Mark Recognition (OMR) (see Figure 2.2);
► Optical Character Recognition (OCR);
► bar codes (see Figure 2.3);
► magnetic stripe card (see Figure 2.4); etc.

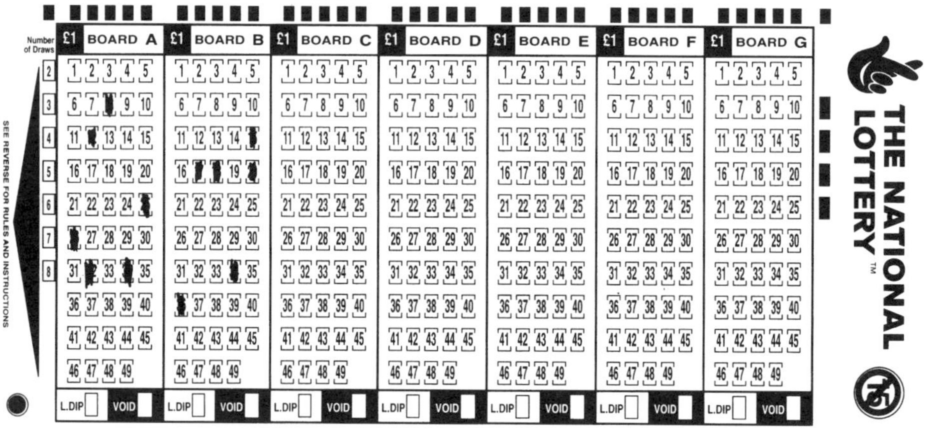

Figure 2.2
A national lottery
payslip uses OMR

Figure 2.3
A bar code used in
a supermarket

Figure 2.4
A magnetic
stripe card

The accuracy and integrity of information

Verification

Verification is checking that the data captured is accurately input to a computer. Information input using a keyboard, from questionnaires or other forms, should be verified. The **double entry** method is commonly used to verify information input using a keyboard. Typically, the information written on a form is typed into the computer twice by different people. The computer checks that they have both entered the same information. If they have not, a mistake has been made and this must be corrected. Double-entry verification ensures accurate input but takes longer and costs more. Consequently, it is avoided if possible.

Validation

Validation is checking that the data captured is reasonable, for example:

- a **length check** checks that a field is not too long or too short;
- a **type check** checks that the information in a field is of the correct data type;
- a **table look-up** checks that, for example, an identification number is one that is in use;
- a **range check** checks that information is in the expected range, for example, that the month number (MM) lies between 1 and 12 inclusive;
- a **check digit** is re-calculated to ensure that, for example, a bar code has been read accurately by a bar code reader.

Keeping information up-to-date and secure

The information on a database has to be kept up-to-date and secure. To do this, you:

- **edit** or **amend** the information stored in a field if it changes;
- **insert** or **create** a new record to add new information to a file;
- **delete** a record to remove it if it is no longer needed;
- **backup** the database by making another copy of it;
- **restore** the database from the backup copy if you lose the original.

What a database can do

Using a database, you can:

- Keep records of customers, criminals, books, stock, pupils, houses for sale, etc.
- Use a **search condition** to find the information you want. An example of a search condition is: Customer_Number is '034736' AND Post_Code is 'BD10 3PY'. It is not unusual to find that information is made available in a form that allows it to be searched using search conditions similar to those used to search a database. For example, the information stored on **CD-ROM** or in an on-line library catalogue.
- **Sort** the information into some order. For example, descending alphabetic order, i.e. Z to A.
- **Select** the information (fields) to include in your report from the information (records) you have found.
- Print a **report** containing the information selected.
- **Export** the results of a search to another piece of software. For example, to a wordprocessor for inclusion in a report.
- **Import** text, images, etc. from other software. For example, a picture of someone to accompany information held as text.

Teletext

- **Teletext**, e.g. Ceefax, is a simple way of handling information using a page-based system.
- Teletext **pages** can be received and displayed on a TV or using a computer.
- Pages are **broadcast in cycle**. You may have to wait until the page you want is broadcast.
- You select teletext pages by typing in their **page number** on a remote control hand set.
- Teletext is not **interactive**. The information you can enter is very limited.
- When a teletext receiver has **fastext**, several pages next to the selected page are stored in memory. You can then access these pages much faster. Other pages are not accessed any faster.
- A **computer** with a teletext receiver can be used to save and print pages.

▶ A teletext **emulator** is software that lets a computer present information in the same way as broadcast teletext. This is useful where people need to be able to get at information using a system they already understand. For example, teletext emulators are often used to provide information in Tourist Information Centres.

The Internet and the World Wide Web

The Internet

The **Internet** is a worldwide collection of interconnected networks. There is no one central organization that owns or controls the Internet or the information on it. It can include the telephone network. It can be used to send, receive and exchange information, nationally and internationally. This facility is developed to provide services, such as **electronic mail** (e-mail) and information services.
To connect to the Internet from home, you will need a modem, a telephone line, and a subscription to an Internet Service Provider

An **Internet Service Provider** (ISP) provides dial-in lines so that users can connect to the Internet. It may also supply additional services. For example, the Internet service provider, America Online (AOL), gives subscribers access to the Internet and provides information about the weather, travel, sport, entertainment, and news.

The World Wide Web

The **World Wide Web** (WWW, the Web, W3) runs over the Internet. It gives you access to an extensive range of information and services, using standard GUIs, and multimedia.

The information is stored on **information servers** (Web sites, Web servers) located throughout the world. You can access the WWW using a **browser**, such as Netscape. This lets you look at the information stored on Web servers (see Figure 2.5).

Figure 2.5
The World Wide Web page at the University of Huddersfield, School of Education

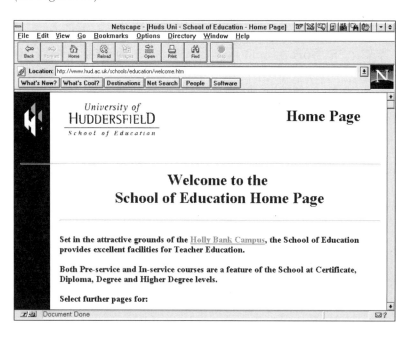

To find information on the WWW, you could:
▶ Access a particular information server using its **Uniform Resource Locator** (URL). This is the address of the Web server. For example, http://www.open.gov.uk is the address of the government's information server.
▶ Use a **search engine**, such as Altavista or Yahoo, to search for particular topics. You enter a search condition and the search engine will look for the information that meets your needs. A search engine will allow you to search the entire WWW using commands similar to those used to interrogate a database.

▶ **Surf** the WWW by activating **hotspots**. Most information servers have hotspots that will connect you to other information servers. These are words, icons or pictures that have been highlighted to indicate that they will give you access to other information or Web sites. This is not always a quick or efficient means of finding information.

★ REVISION ACTIVITIES

Question 1

Tick **three** boxes to show the tasks that can be done using a database.

	Tick three boxes
A 3-D model can be constructed.	
CD-ROMs can be sent through the post with little risk that the information stored on them will be corrupted.	
Information about a car's owner can be accessed from a moving police car by typing in the car's registration number.	
At an estate agents, a list of houses that meet a client's needs can be quickly found and printed.	
An overall summary of a school's GCSE results can be made very quickly from records of each pupil's results.	
A laser printer produces a higher quality printout than a dot matrix printer.	

Question 2

The data stored in a database is often coded.
   Which of the following statements is true?

1 Data is coded so that spies cannot understand it.
2 If you were coding the names of towns, 10/2P would be a better code for Leeds than LS.
3 Data is coded to save storage space.
4 You should always code peoples' names.
5 Dates are coded in YYMMDD form because it is easier to sort them into chronological order.

Question 3

This information is part of a database used by a tennis club:

Member_ Number	Name	Member_ Category	Subscription_ Outstanding (£)
237	Jones, Paul	Full	34.50
098	Jackson, Jean	Student	3.00
035	Majid, Rizwan	Student	4.50
119	Kosar, Roksana	Full	25.00
099	Robinson, Martin	Honorary	0.00
876	Rodin, Selvar	Full	17.00

(a) Write down the Member_Number(s) of the records selected by these search conditions.

Search condition	Member_Number(s) of records selected
Name begins with 'K'.	
Member_Number contains '9'.	
Subscription_Outstanding is more than 20.00.	
Name begins with 'R' AND Member_Category is Full.	
Member_Category is NOT Honorary.	
Name begins with 'J' OR Member_Category is Honorary.	

(b) Write down members' names after the records have been sorted into descending order on the Subscription_Outstanding field.
(c) Design a suitable coding system for the Member_Category field.
(d) Design a form for members to fill in when they join the tennis club.
(e) Describe a suitable validation check for the Member_Number field.

Question 4
(a) Write down three different types of information that can be accessed using teletext.
(b) Name a teletext service.
(c) Describe how you access information on teletext.
(d) State one advantage and one disadvantage of teletext.

Question 5
(a) What is the Internet? Explain how you could connect to the Internet.
(b) Write down three different types of information that can be accessed on the World Wide Web.
(c) Describe three ways you can find information on the WWW.

PRACTICE QUESTIONS

Question 1
(a) Ring **three** items that could be found in a database.

    a field   a name
    a heat sensor   a printer
    a mouse   a scanned image

(b) Tick **three** boxes to show the advantages of using a database to handle a large volume of information.

	Tick three boxes
You can quickly search the information to find out what you want to know.	
Databases are not used to store large volumes of information.	

continued

Databases are easier to use than photocopiers.	
The space needed to store a large volume of information on a database is much less than if it was written down.	
Large volumes of information stored on a database can be copied and sent around the world much faster and at less cost than on paper.	
You can easily search a database but it may not tell you what you want to know.	

Question 2

A date is coded in YYMMDD form. For example, 790611 is the 11th June 1979.

(a) Write down the codes for these dates:
   (i)   12th February 1985.
   (ii) 6th December 2000.
(b) Write down the dates for these codes:
   (i)   970113.
   (ii) 451013.
(c) Why are these date codes invalid? Give reasons for your answers.
   (i)   871301.
   (ii) 791232.
   (iii) 260231.

Question 3

(a) Tick **two** boxes to show which of the following statements about teletext are true.

	Tick two boxes
You access information on teletext by entering a page number.	
You can use search conditions to find information.	
You may have to wait for the page you want as they are broadcast in cycle.	
Teletext pages contain high quality video clips.	
You have to pay an annual fee to use teletext.	

(b) What is fastext? Is it always faster? Explain your answer.
(c) State two advantages in using a computer to access teletext instead of a TV.

Question 4

An IT system is used in a small library to control the lending of books to members.

(a) Describe the records that would be used in the database files.
(b) Design forms to be filled in when:
   (i)   new members join the library;
   (ii) members request a book that they want to borrow that is not in the library.

(c) Design a library membership card.

(d) Describe one verification check that might be used.

(e) Describe one validation check that might be used.

(f) Describe one report the librarian would want printing, and say why the information in the report is needed.

(g) (i) Describe one possible effect if the information stored on the database was incorrect.

    (ii) Describe one way the library could find out if the information stored on the database was correct.

Question 5

This table shows a part of a school's database of information about pupils.

Pupil_ Number	Name	Sex	Form	Days_ Absent	Area	Health
2045	Jackson, P	M	7EG	0	Thornton	good
2001	Singh, R	M	8WE	5	Allerton	good
1874	Dean, N	M	9GH	3	Allerton	epilepsy
1045	Dobson, J	M	7EG	2	Allerton	good
1057	Ellis, M	M	10RT	0	Bingley	good
0056	Patel, M	M	9GH	9	Denholme	asthma
2343	Grant, K	F	9GH	14	Queensbury	asthma
4892	Wall, R	F	8WE	11	Thornton	good

(a) Using words from the list complete the sentences.

    alphanumeric   pupil
    eight   seven
    numeric   teacher

- The database file has one record for every ....
- In each record, the number of fields shown is ....
- The data type of the Name field is ....

(b) (i) Write down the fieldname of the key field.

    (ii) Why is a key field used?

    (iii) When a new pupil's details are entered, the database generates the key field. Why is this?

(c) (i) Design a code for the Health field.

    (ii) Give two advantages in using a code.

    (iii) When new pupils start at the school, they have to fill in a form. Using a diagram, explain how information about a pupil's state of health would be collected on this form.

(d) (i) Describe a validation check that could be done on the Sex field.

    (ii) Describe two different validation checks that could be done on the Pupil_Number field.

(e) Write down the names of pupils in the order they would appear after the records have been sorted into:

    (i) Ascending order on the Name field.

    (ii) Descending order on the Pupil_Number field.

(f) Write down the names of pupils who are selected using these search conditions. *
     is a wild card.
     (i)   Health is NOT 'good'.   (v)   Form is '7EG' OR Area is 'Thornton'.
     (ii)   Sex is NOT 'M'.   (vi)   Health is 'Epilepsy' OR Sex is 'F'.
     (iii) Sex is 'M' AND Form is   (vii) Form is '7EG' AND Days Absent is
            '*WE'.   NOT bigger than 2.
     (iv)   Name begins with 'D' AND   (viii) (Form is '9GH' AND Sex is 'M') OR
            Form is '7EG'.   Area is 'Queensbury'.

(g) Write **search conditions** that will find the answers to the following questions.
     You should say who might need this information; in what order the records should
     be printed; and name the fields that should be printed.
     (i)   Which pupils are boys?   (v)   Which girls are in 9GH?
     (ii)   Which boys have been absent   (vi)   Which boys are in 7EG?
            from school for more than 3 days?   (vii) Which pupils are in good health?
     (iii) Which pupils live in Allerton?   (viii) Which pupils who live in Denholme
     (iv)   Which pupils who live in   have asthma?
            Allerton have been absent for   (ix)   Which pupils live in Queensbury or
            more than 3 days?   Denholme?

(h) (i)   Describe one possible effect if the information stored on the database was incorrect.
     (ii)   Describe one way the school could find out if the information stored on the
            database was correct.

Question 6

(a) (i)   Describe a method of double-entry verification.
     (ii)   What is the purpose of verification?
     (iii) Describe one advantage of this method.
     (iv)   Describe one disadvantage of this method.
(b) (i)   Describe one validation check that could be used on a date coded in
            YYMMDD form.
     (ii)   Describe one validation check that could be used when a bar code is read.
     (iii) Describe one validation check that could be used to ensure a credit card can
            be used.

Question 7

(a) Name two different teletext services.
(b) Write down six different types of information that can be accessed using teletext.
(c) For two different types of information, give an example of who might want to
     access it and why they might want to access it.
(d) You can access information by typing in its page number. Describe how you
     would do this.
(e) There can be a long time between entering the page number and when the page is
     displayed. Why is this?
(f) (i)   What is fastext?
     (ii)   Why is fastext faster?
     (iii) Sometimes fastext isn't any faster. Why not?
(g) Is teletext interactive? Give reasons for your answer.
(h) Using a computer with a teletext card, investors can download share prices from
     teletext, and analyse them. State one advantage and one disadvantage of doing this.

Question 8

(a) What is the Internet?
(b) Describe the hardware, software and other services that would be needed to
     connect a desk top PC to the Internet.

(c) What is the World Wide Web?

(d) (i)   Write down three different types of information that can be accessed on the World Wide Web.

    (ii)   Name three WWW sites and write down their URLs.

    (iii) State one advantage and one disadvantage of using URLs to access WWW sites.

(e) (i)   Describe how you would use a search engine to find information on the WWW.

    (ii)   State one advantage and one disadvantage of using a search engine to find information on the WWW.

(f) (i)   What is surfing?

    (ii)   State one advantage and one disadvantage of surfing the WWW to find information.

    (iii) State one reason why parents might want to control their children's access to the WWW.

Question 9

VANTEC is an international agency that arranges the transport of a wide range of goods.

VANTEC uses a database to store information about goods being transported.

(a) This is part of the information stored on the database:

Trip number	Cargo	Departs from	Type of transport
023	machine tools	Coventry	container
154	meal	Skipton	bulk carrier
157	methanol	Liverpool	tanker
205	methanol	Plymouth	tanker
347	clothing	Newcastle	container
539	meat	London	cool store

   – A database user is trying to find all the records that relate to the transport of methanol.

   – The user types in this search condition: {Find **Cargo** starts with 'm'}.

   – The database displays all the records that relate to the transport of machine tools, meal, meat, methanol and some other cargoes.

   (i)   Complete the sentence to give the **shortest** search condition that will find the records that relate to the transport of methanol but not those that relate to the transport of machine tools, meal and meat.

      Search condition: {Find **Cargo** starts with ....}   [1]

   (ii)   Explain why the search condition you have given does **not** find those records that relate to the transport of machine tools, meal and meat.   [1]

   (iii) Explain why the search condition you have given may still **not** select only those records that relate to the transport of methanol.   [1]

(b) A database user wants to find all the records that relate to the transport of meat and meal. Only **one** cargo is carried on a trip.

   (i)   Explain why this search condition will **not** find all the records that relate to the transport of meat and meal.

      Search condition: {Find **Cargo** is 'meat' AND **Cargo** is 'Meal'}   [1]

   (ii)   Write a search condition that **will** find all the records that relate to the transport of meat and meal.   [1]

(c) VANTEC wants to build a new freight terminal with a high speed rail link to the Channel Tunnel.

VANTEC wants to find out what people think about it building this new freight terminal.

VANTEC designs a suitable questionnaire and conducts a survey to collect information.

(i) Describe how the information collected could be analysed using Information Technology. [4]

SEG

Question 10

In a Job Centre, a database is used to hold data about the jobs available. Here is one of the displays that the database can produce:

Job Ref	Employer	Minimum age	Minimum qualifications	Pay (£ per year)	Type of job	Area
Ecc/234	NEAB	23	2 GCSE	6745	Clerical	Eccles
Ecc/748	Widget	16	2 GCSE	5723	Clerical	Eccles
Liv/348	Music Inc.	25	3 years exp.	18567	Sales	Liverpool
Orp/548	Sam Travel	21	4 GCSE	10027	Driver	Orpington
Man/345	A 1 Marketing	18	4 GCSE	12000	Sales	Manchester
Hal/839	JJ Racing	116	None	6440	Manual	Halifax

(a) (i) Look closely at the information shown above. **Circle** the **one** piece of data that is obviously a mistake. [1]

(ii) Say why this is a mistake. [1]

(b) Give **three** advantages of using this type of computer database to search for particular jobs rather than looking through all the jobs on cards pinned to the walls. [3]

Queries for this system are written like this:
– Minimum age > = 21
– Minimum age < 18 AND Area = 'Manchester'

(c) Write down the query you would use to search for all jobs which pay more than £10,000 per year. [3]

(d) Write down the query you would use to search the database for all the jobs for people 18 or over in sales which pay more than £13,000. [5]

NEAB

Modelling and spreadsheets

Remember, in a spreadsheet:

▶ what is meant by a **row**, a **column**, a **cell**;
▶ that cells can contain text, numbers, formulae, dates and times;
▶ that cell references can refer to one cell or a range of cells;
▶ that cell references can be relative or absolute;
▶ that formulae recalculate automatically.

Do not just remember facts. If possible, make sure you can use a spreadsheet:

▶ to organize and display information;
▶ to generate graphs;
▶ for modelling.

Make sure you can:

▶ load and save a spreadsheet;
▶ enter information into cells and edit it;
▶ format cells for integers or money;
▶ centre, left justify and right justify cells;
▶ move or copy cells;

▶ insert and delete, rows and columns;
▶ sort rows;
▶ generate bar, pie, and line graphs;
▶ export a range of cells or a graph;
▶ print a range of cells or a graph.

Spreadsheets

A **spreadsheet** (see Figure 3.1) can be used for the wide variety of tasks that involve calculations laid out in rows and columns. For example, they are often used for financial applications and in mathematics.

Figure 3.1
Using a spreadsheet

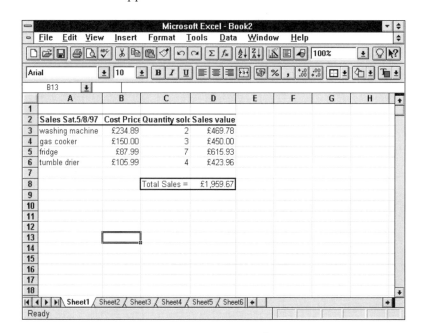

Cells

▶ A spreadsheet is divided into horizontal **rows** and vertical **columns** (see Figure 3.2).

▶ A **cell** is the intersection of a row and a column.

▶ The **active cell** is the cell that is currently highlighted by the cursor or mouse pointer.

Figure 3.2
A spreadsheet divided into rows and columns

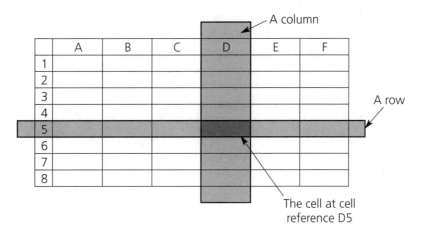

Cell contents

The **contents** of a cell can contain different types of information. For example:

▶ **text**, e.g. Mr. Jones.

▶ **numbers**, e.g. 23, £34.67.

▶ **formulae**, e.g. SUM(A2:A11).

▶ **dates**, e.g. 20/11/96.

▶ **times**, e.g. 09:38:04 PM.

Cell references

▶ **Cell references** can refer to individual cells. For example, the cell with cell reference D5 (see Figure 3.2).

▶ A cell reference can be a **relative cell reference**. This will adjust automatically when it is moved or copied to a new position. For example, suppose the formula SUM(D3:D9) is in cell D10. If this formula is moved from D10 to H10, the formula will change to SUM(H3:H9). As D3 and D9 are relative cell references, they change.

▶ A cell reference can be an **absolute cell reference**. This will not change when it is moved or copied to a new position. For example, suppose A1 is the absolute cell reference for cell A1, and the formula C3*A1 is in cell D3. If this formula is moved from D3 to D4, the formula will change to C4*A1. As A1 is an absolute cell reference, it does not change.

▶ A **cell range reference** refers to a group of cells. For example: the cell range reference B2:D7 refers to the rectangular block of cells with B2 in the top left-hand corner and D7 in the bottom right-hand corner (see Figure 3.3).

Figure 3.3
A cell range reference

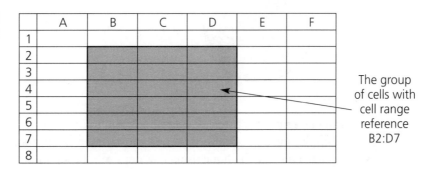

What spreadsheets can do

▶ **Formulae** may **recalculate automatically** when the numbers in the cells they refer to change. For example, SUM(B3:B6) may recalculate automatically if the values in any of the cells B3, B4, B5 or B6 change.

▶ Cells can be **moved** or **copied** from one part of the spreadsheet to another.

▶ Rows and columns can be **deleted**, that is, taken out; and **inserted**, that is put in.

▶ **Formats** can be applied to individual cells, rows, columns or the whole spreadsheet. For example, a column that contains amounts of money could be formatted so that the numbers in it always have a £ symbol on the left-hand side and show only two decimal places, e.g. £9.37.

▶ It is possible to **sort** groups of cells. For example, the rows may be sorted so that names in column A are in alphabetic order.

▶ You can generate **graphs** that illustrate the information stored in the spreadsheet. For example, bar charts, pie charts and line graphs can be generated (see Figures 3.4, 3.5 and 3.6).

Figure 3.4
A bar chart

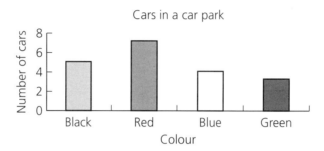

Figure 3.5
A line graph

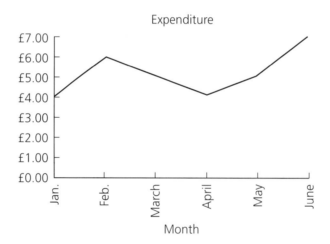

Figure 3.6
A pie chart

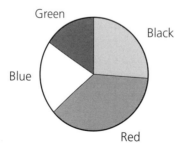

▶ You can **export** a range of cells or a graph to another piece of software. For example, a group of cells could be exported to a wordprocessor for inclusion in a report. This may be done using cut, copy and paste operations, as follows:
1. In the spreadsheet, highlight the cells to be exported, and copy them.
2. In the wordprocessor, paste the cells.

Modelling

A **model** is a representation of the real world. It is not the real world. It can be used to:

▶ improve understanding of a well known situation;
▶ learn about unfamiliar situations;
▶ increase awareness and understanding of the situation modelled;
▶ help understand problems and try out different solutions;
▶ experiment without danger or expense;
▶ predict what will happen.

Modelling using a spreadsheet

Spreadsheets can be used for modelling though they are more often used to handle information. A spreadsheet model will:

▶ allow a range of input variables to be set;
▶ use formulae to define the rules on which the model is based;
▶ output information using the input variables, stored values, and the rules.

REVISION ACTIVITIES

Question 1
Using words from the list, complete the sentences.

buildings	cellophane	pavements
cell	columns	rows

– A spreadsheet is divided into horizontal .... and vertical
....
– The intersection of a row and a column is a ....

Question 2
Ring **all** those words that describe the information that can be entered into a cell.

cell reference	model	times	menu	dates
text	formulae	equation	printer	numbers

Question 3
Tick **three** boxes to show which of the following statements are true.

	Tick three boxes
Relative cell references will adjust automatically when formulae are copied from one cell to another.	
A spreadsheet is unlikely to have more than 10 columns and 20 rows.	
Graphs generated by a spreadsheet cannot be printed.	
Formulae may recalculate automatically when the numbers in the cells they refer to change.	
An absolute cell reference will not change when it is moved or copied to a new position.	
The contents of a cell cannot be changed.	

Question 4

A teacher uses a spreadsheet to analyse pupils' examination results. This is part of the spreadsheet.

	A	B	C	D	E
1	**Student**	**English**	**Maths**	**Science**	**Average**
2	Dobson	50	56	45	50.3
3	Harris	44	34	42	40.0
4	Singh	70	67	68	68.3
5	Patel	57	23	45	41.7
6	Edwards	55	54	53	54.0
7	Sweryt	65	52	62	59.7
8	**Average**	56.8	47.7	52.5	

(a) Write down the cell reference of a cell that could contain:
  (i) Text.
  (ii) Numbers.
(b) Write down the formulae that would be in cell E3.
(c) Rows 2 to 7 are sorted into ascending order on the students' names in column A.
    Write down these rows after they have been sorted.
(d) Put these statements in order to show how the teacher could include a graph in a
    report about the examinations.
       paste the graph
       highlight the graph
       run the wordprocessor
       run the spreadsheet
       copy the graph
(e) Give one advantage in using a spreadsheet to analyse this information.

Question 5

DRIVEIT is an arcade game that simulates driving a car on a race track.

(a) Describe two ways information could be input to DRIVEIT.
(b) Tick **three** boxes to show the rules that would be built into DRIVEIT.

	Tick three boxes
If the driver is under 25, insurance premiums are much lower.	
If a car runs out of petrol, the game is over.	
There are five cars on the track at the start of the game.	
If a car leaves the track, it crashes.	
If a car crashes four times, the game is over.	
The driver can see the track from different viewpoints behind the car's seat.	

(c) Describe one way playing DRIVEIT could help a learner driver.

PRACTICE QUESTIONS

Question 1

(a) Ring **three** types of information that could be entered into a cell in a spreadsheet.

debit card   number

formula   text

joystick   wordprocessor

(b) Ring **three** types of information that can be output from a spreadsheet.

algorithms   keyboards

bar charts   pie charts

calculations   printers

(c) Tick **three** boxes to show the tasks that can be done using a spreadsheet.

	Tick three boxes
Constructing a predator/prey model.	
Working out the cost of making a cake.	
Arranging trees systematically.	
Reporting on the profits made by a business.	
Models can be made out of plastic or card.	
Scanning and editing photographs.	

(d) Describe **three** advantages of using a spreadsheet.

(e) Describe **three** disadvantages of using a spreadsheet.

Question 2

This spreadsheet shows the value of sales from a school tuck shop over a three week period.

	A	B	C	D
1		**Week 1**	**Week 2**	**Week 3**
2	**Mon**	33.78	34.64	30.75
3	**Tue**	7.65	6.05	3.16
4	**Wed**	27.65	28.95	22.45
5	**Thur**	40.50	39.75	36.41
6	**Fri**	33.79	35.85	30.75
7				
8	**Totals**	143.37	145.24	123.52

(a) Write down the cell reference of a cell that would contain:

(i) Text.

(ii) Numbers.

(b) Write down the formulae that would be in cell C8.

(c) When it is open, the tuck shop takes about £25 at lunch time. On which day is the tuck shop closed at lunch time?

(d) Give one reason why a spreadsheet should be used in this case.

(e) Give one reason why a spreadsheet should not be used in this case.

Question 3

At the end of each week, a shopkeeper uses a spreadsheet to record what has been sold. This is part of the spreadsheet.

	A	B	C	D	E	F	G
1	**Week ending**	**14/11/97**					
2	**Goods**	**Cost price**	**Selling price**	**Number sold**	**Value of sales**	**Profit**	**%Profit**
3	**Cereals**						
4	Muesli	1.70	1.95	85	165.75	21.25	12.8
5	Porridge	0.80	0.90	65	58.50	6.50	11.1
6	Corn Flakes	0.78	1.05	124	130.20	33.48	25.7
7	Bran Flakes	0.85	0.95	53	50.35	5.30	10.5
8				**Totals=**	404.80	66.53	

(a) Write down the formulae that would be in these cells:

(i) E5.   (iv) F8.

(ii) E8.   (v) G4.

(iii) F6.

(b) Describe one possible effect if the information entered into the spreadsheet was incorrect.

(c) Rows 4 to 7 are to be sorted into ascending order on the names of the cereals in column A.

(i) Write down rows 4 to 7 after this sort has been done.

(ii) Describe one precaution that should be taken before sorting the rows of a spreadsheet.

(d) (i) Draw a graph that the shopkeeper could generate from the information shown using the spreadsheet.

(ii) Explain how the graph would be useful to the shopkeeper.

(iii) The shopkeeper is writing a report using a wordprocessor. Describe how the graph could be included in this report.

(e) State one advantage and one disadvantage to the shopkeeper of using a spreadsheet to record sales.

Question 4

This spreadsheet shows how much interest will be earned on a savings account over a three year period.

	A	B	C	D
1	Rate of interest	5 per cent		
2				
3		**Year 1**	**Year 2**	**Year 3**
4	Amount saved	£200.00	£210.00	£220.50
5	Annual interest	£10.00	£10.50	£11.03
6	End of year total	£210.00	£220.50	£231.53

(a) Write down the cell references of two cells that would contain:

(i) Text.

(ii) Numbers.

(b) Identify one input variable, and give its cell reference.
(c) Explain why references to cell B1 are likely to be absolute cell references.
(d) Write down the formulae that would be in cell D6.
(e) Write down the formulae that would be in cell C4.
(f) Write down the formulae that would be in cell B5. Clearly show which cell references are relative cell references and which are absolute cell references.
(g) The spreadsheet assumes that the rate of interest stays the same for 3 years. Is this a reasonable assumption? Give a reason for your answer.
(h) Describe how you would export the cells with cell range reference A1:D6 to a report being prepared using a wordprocessor.

Question 5
A computer-based flight simulator is used to train pilots.
Tick **three** boxes to show which of the following statements are true.

	Tick three boxes
Using a flight simulator is more dangerous than flying an aeroplane.	
A flight simulator could be used to learn to fly an aeroplane.	
Passengers will get to their destinations faster on a flight simulator.	
A pilot could use a flight simulator to see how an aeroplane would perform in different weather conditions.	
A flight simulator could be used to see what it is like to fly different aeroplanes.	
Flight simulators are more expensive to run than the space shuttle.	

Question 6
An insecticide is used to kill the insects that attack crops. A farmer uses a computer-based model to work out how much of the insecticide to spray.

(a) One unfortunate side-effect of spraying this insecticide is that it reduces the quality of the crop. This means that one rule built into the model is: 'As the amount of insecticide sprayed goes up, the quality of the crop goes down'. Using outcomes from the list complete the trends to make other rules that would be built into the model.

Outcomes
– the number of insects killed goes up.
– the colour of the crop changes to purple.
– the crop yield goes up.
– the soil quality improves.
– the soil temperature increases.

Trends
– As the amount of insecticide sprayed goes up, ...
– As the number of insects attacking the crop goes down, ...
(b) Describe one way in which using this model could help the farmer.
(c) Describe one way in which using this model might not help the farmer.

Question 7
A DIY superstore uses a computer-based model to decide how many point of sale checkouts to use.

(a) Describe a manual method and an automatic method of telling the computer how many checkouts are in use.

(b) Tick **three** boxes to show what assumptions would be made about how the model operates.

	Tick three boxes
All the checkout operators work at the same speed all the time.	
All the customers go to one checkout.	
The superstore gives a 20 per cent discount on a Tuesday and a Thursday.	
Some customers take longer to go through the checkout as they have bought more goods.	
All the checkouts in use can be operated at the same speed.	
Equal numbers of customers queue at each checkout.	

(c) On average, it takes 4 minutes to serve a customer.
   (i) Work out the shortest time the last customer in the queue will have to wait if there are 3 checkouts in use and 21 customers waiting.
  (ii) Work out the shortest time the last customer in the queue will have to wait if there are 5 checkouts in use and 20 customers waiting.

(d) Describe a manual method and an automatic method of working out the average time to serve a customer.

(e) Show how this model could be constructed using a spreadsheet. You should clearly state any formulae used.

Question 8

(a) A hospital uses a fleet of ambulances.
The hospital uses a computer-based model of the surrounding area to decide which ambulance should go to an emergency.
  (i) This is part of the map of the surrounding area the model displays. The numbers are the average time in minutes for an ambulance to travel that section of the map.

Figure 3.7

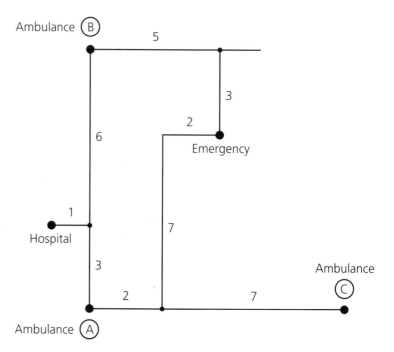

Which ambulance should the hospital send to the emergency? [1]

(ii) Tick **two** boxes to show the information the model should provide to help the hospital decide which ambulance to send. [2]

	Tick two boxes
The time it will take for each ambulance to get to the emergency.	
The distance each ambulance will have to travel to get to the emergency.	
The name of the patient.	
The amount of petrol the ambulance will use.	
An indication whether the medical supplies carried will allow an ambulance to deal with the emergency.	

(iii) The model has to make some assumptions about the ambulances.
For example, the model assumes that all the ambulance drivers are fully trained.
Describe **two** other assumptions the model would make. [2]

(b) A spreadsheet is used to manage the medical supplies carried by an ambulance.
This is part of the spreadsheet:

	A	B	C	D	E
1	Description of items	Unit cost	Quantity		
2	stretchers	707.50	2	1415.00	
3	bandages	2.00	50	100.00	
4	medicines	5.50	40	220.00	
5					
6			Total value=	1735.00	
7					

(i)   Write a formula that will work out the value in cell D3. [1]
(ii) Write a formula that will work out the value in cell D6. [1]
(iii) Complete these sentences, using terms from the list. [3]

      a byte   a matrix
      a cable   a number
      a formula   text

   – Cell B2 contains ....
   – Cell C6 contains ....
   – The value of .... may be re-calculated when the value of a number in a cell is changed.

(iv) It is decided to reduce the total value of the medical supplies carried by an ambulance to below £1400.
Explain how the spreadsheet could be used to decide what medical supplies will be carried. [3]

(c) The computer-based model and the spreadsheet are separate information systems.
The hospital wants to integrate all its information systems. A systems analyst is asked to carry out a **feasibility study**.

Complete the sentences, using terms from the list.

buildings	reports
costs	stores
problems	

– The systems analyst finds out what the .... are by talking to users.
– The systems analyst looks at all the possible ways of integrating these information systems and works out the .... of each option.
– The systems analyst .... the findings of the feasibility study to management.

SEG

Question 9

A hotel wants to organize a disco and wishes to know the minimum number of tickets it must sell to make a profit. The hotel manager has created the spreadsheet shown in Figure 3.8 in order to help find this out.
Study the spreadsheet carefully and answer the following questions

(a) In Figure 3.8 how many tickets must be sold for the hotel to *first* make a profit? [1]
(b) The manager used formulae to work out the Total Cost and the Profit. Write down suitable formulae which he might have used.
   (i) Formula for TOTAL COST. [1]
   (ii) Formula for PROFIT. [1]
(c) The manager wants to increase profits by increasing the price of tickets. An existing ticket costs £18.00 and the new cost is £20.00. The manager makes changes in the ticket costs in Column B.
   Which column data will also change as a result of the manager's actions? [1]
(d) Give **one** other example of how a *different* spreadsheet can be used in the hotel. [1]
(e) State **two** advantages of using the spreadsheet in the example you have given in part (d) of this question. [2]

WJEC

Figure 3.8

	A	B	C	D	E	F	G	H
1			ANALYSIS OF DISCO COST					
2								
3	**No of tickets sold**	**Cost of one ticket**	**Income**	**Music hire**	**BBQ cost**	**Printing cost**	**Total costs**	**Profit**
4	0	18	0	100	0	200	300	−300
5	5	18	90	100	10	200	310	−220
6	15	18	270	100	30	200	330	−60
7	25	18	450	100	50	200	350	100
8	35	18	630	100	70	200	370	260
9	45	18	810	100	90	200	390	420
10	55	18	990	100	110	200	410	580
11	65	18	1170	100	130	200	430	740
12	75	18	1350	100	150	200	450	900
13	85	18	1530	100	170	200	470	1060
14	95	18	1710	100	190	200	490	1220
15	105	18	1890	100	210	200	510	1380

4 *Monitoring and control*

Remember what is meant by:

▶ a sensor;
▶ an actuator;
▶ data logging;
▶ the frequency of sampling;
▶ the period of logging;
▶ a dedicated control system;
▶ a computer control system;
▶ feedback.

Remember that:

▶ a computer program is a list of instructions;
▶ a computer program is written in a computer language, such as BASIC, Logo or Pascal;
▶ a flowchart describes how a task is done or a computer program is constructed.

Do not just remember facts. If possible, make sure you have:

▶ done an experiment using data logging;
▶ used a computer control language;
▶ built a model of a computer control system;
▶ written a program in a computer language, such as BASIC, Logo or Pascal.

Make sure you can use these types of structure in a computer program:

▶ conditional statements;
▶ loops;
▶ procedures.

TOPIC OUTLINE

Sensors and actuators

▶ A **sensor** is an input device used to measure environmental conditions. Different sensors can monitor temperature, humidity, light, sound, pressure, wind speed, wind direction, tilt, etc.
▶ An **actuator** is an output device used to adjust environmental conditions. Actuators are heaters, motors, valves, pumps, boilers, etc. Their **source of power** could be electricity, hydraulics, compressed air, etc.

Data logging

Data logging is the automatic recording and storage of the information provided by sensors. For example, a weather station may automatically record and store the temperature once every hour. Where there are a number of weather stations distributed over wide distances, perhaps in remote locations, the information stored could be automatically downloaded to a central computer over the telecommunications network.

Frequency of sampling

The **frequency of sampling** or **time interval** gives the time between measurements. This affects the amount of information available, and may alter our view of the situation. If the time interval is too long, there may not be enough information; if it is too short there may be too much. For example, in an experiment a scientist is investigating how a cup of coffee cools after it has been heated in a microwave oven. If the frequency of sampling is one measurement per hour (time interval = 1 hour), this will not provide enough information as the cup of coffee will have returned to room temperature after 1 hour. One measurement every 10 seconds would be better as there would be more measurements taken when the coffee is actually cooling so that the scientist can see what is happening. Taking measurements every half second would provide much more information but it is unlikely to change the view the scientist has of the cooling process. Consequently, this is unnecessary.

Period of logging

The **period of logging** is the length of time the logging takes place. For example, a cup of coffee that has been heated in a microwave will cool to room temperature in about 10 minutes. In this case it is pointless continuing taking measurements beyond 10 minutes. The period of logging is 10 minutes.

Control systems

Control systems monitor and control environmental conditions using sensors to determine what is happening, and actuators to change what is happening. Examples are central heating control systems, robots, flight simulators, greenhouse control systems, and automated warehousing and manufacturing systems, etc.

Feedback

Feedback is a cycle of sensing, processing and reaction. In control systems, feedback is an essential process. For example, a central heating control system uses a thermostat to sense the temperature. If the temperature is too low it activates the boiler to provide heat and opens valves to allow heat to flow through the system; if the temperature is too high it switches off the boiler and closes the valves to reduce the heat. Without feedback the central heating control system would not know if heat was required. As a result, it could provide heat when it is already hot enough, or not provide heat when it is cold.

Types of control systems

▶ **Dedicated control systems** are built into equipment, for example, in a domestic washing machine.
▶ **Computer control systems** are computer based, and typically communicate with sensors and actuators using a control interface. A **control interface** (see Figure 4.1) is the hardware that converts the signals from the sensors so that the computer can understand them and the signals from the computer so that the actuators can understand them. Computer control systems are more flexible as a computer can easily be re-programmed. They are more versatile as the computer can control several different control systems, or be used for other tasks such as wordprocessing, at the same time.

Computer programs

Computers themselves are controlled by **programs**. A computer program is a list of instructions to a computer written in a computer **language**. There are many different computer languages, for example, BASIC, Logo, and Pascal.

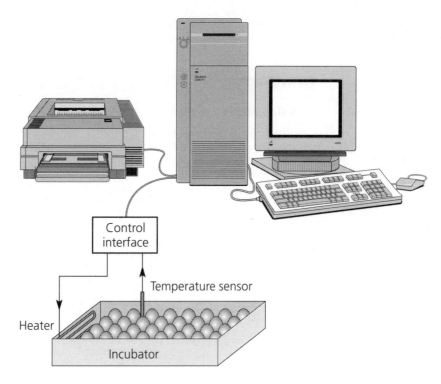

Figure 4.1
A computer control system for an incubator

Computer programming language

▶ A computer language may be designed to initiate a very restricted range of actions, for example, a robot might have a computer control language like this:

```
START
PICK UP BOX FROM PLATFORM A
PLACE BOX ON PLATFORM B
END
```

▶ **General purpose** computer languages are harder to understand but can do a wider range of tasks, for example, BASIC. This is a small program written in BASIC that calculates and outputs the area of a circle after the user has input the radius.

```
10  PRINT "Input the radius of the circle"
20  INPUT Radius
30  Area = 3.14*Radius*Radius
40  PRINT "The area is", Area
50  END
```

Conditional statements, loops and procedures

Different types of **program structure** can be used in a computer program. Examples are:

▶ **Conditional statements** which may change what the program does depending on whether a condition has been satisfied or otherwise.
For example, in BASIC:

```
IF INPUT = "YES" THEN AffirmativeAction ELSE NegativeAction
```

▶ A **loop** is a series of instructions that is repeated.
For example, in Logo:

```
REPEAT 4 [FORWARD 50 LEFT 90]
```

When the instructions in the square brackets are repeated four times, a square is drawn.

▶ A **procedure** is a self-contained sequence of instructions that can be run from elsewhere in the same program.
For example, in Logo, the procedure Polygon is defined by the instructions:

```
TO POLYGON: 'NUMBER' 'SIDE' 'ANGLE'
REPEAT:NUMBER [FORWARD:SIDE LEFT:ANGLE]
END
```

Using this procedure to draw a square, you would use this instruction: POLYGON 4 50 90

Flowcharts

A **flowchart** (see Figure 4.2) can be used to describe how a task is done or a computer program is constructed, for example, this flowchart describes the operation of a simple central heating system.

Figure 4.2
A flowchart showing the operation of a simple central heating system

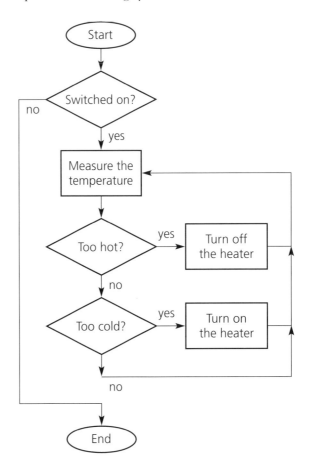

★ REVISION ACTIVITIES

Question 1

Using words from the list complete the sentences.

measure	recording
output	removing
storage	input
adjust	

- A sensor is an .... device used to .... environmental conditions.
- An actuator is an .... device used to .... environmental conditions.
- Data logging is the automatic .... and .... of the information from sensors.

Question 2
Tick **three** boxes to show what could be detected using sensors.

	Tick three boxes
Wind speed.	
Social class.	
Biodiversity.	
Air humidity.	
Soil temperature.	
Leisure pursuit.	

Question 3
Ring the devices that are actuators.

bicycle	electricity	valve	boiler
motor	pram	pump	heater
compressed air	switch	water	horse

Question 4
The computer-controlled robot in Figure 4.3 can pick up objects.
These instructions can be used to control the robot. Only the numbers can be changed.

START	start the program
END	end the program
OPEN	open the claws
CLOSE	close the claws and hold the object
UP 3	raise the claws 3 cm
DOWN 4	lower the claws 4 cm

Figure 4.3

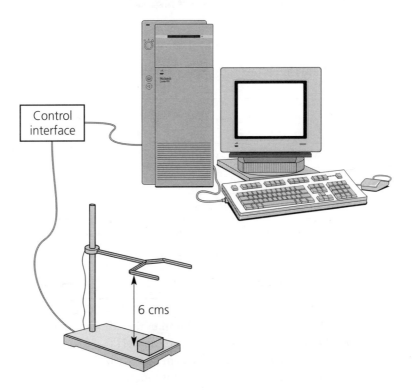

Control interface

6 cms

(a) Put these instructions in order so that starting from the position shown the robot lifts the object 3 cm.

    END
    START
    CLOSE
    DOWN 6
    UP 3
    OPEN

(b) This program is wrong. Describe what would happen when the program is run.

    START
    CLOSE
    DOWN 6
    CLOSE
    DOWN 5
    END

Question 5

Using words from the list, complete the sentences.

minute	10 seconds	3 hours	day
half hour	hour	month	year

- To show how a hot cup of coffee cools, its temperature should be measured once every ....
- To show how the temperature changes during the day, it should be measured once every ....
- To show how the temperature changes during the year, it should be measured once every ....

The time at which the temperature was measured is taken.

All the information is input to a spreadsheet.

PRACTICE QUESTIONS

Question 1

A house is protected by a computer-controlled burglar alarm.

(a) Tick **three** boxes to show which sensors the alarm could use to detect burglars.

	Tick three boxes
Microswitches on windows.	
Springs in furniture.	
Pressure pads under carpets.	
Passive Infra Red detectors (PIRs) mounted on walls.	
Humidity sensors under tables.	
Light sensors in the garden.	

(b) When a sensor detects a burglar, the computer activates a warning signal. Describe two types of warning signal.

(c) Cats can set off burglar alarms. Describe what could be done so that a burglar alarm will detect a burglar but not a cat.

Question 2

A pupil is blindfolded and asked to follow instructions.
You are allowed to use these instructions. Only the numbers can be changed.
    FORWARD 3 PACES
    TURN LEFT 90 DEGREES
    TURN RIGHT 60 DEGREES
    REPEAT 4 TIMES [any of the other instructions]

(a) Draw the shape the pupil would walk round if these instructions were given.
    FORWARD 5 PACES
    TURN LEFT 90 DEGREES
    FORWARD 2 PACES
    TURN LEFT 90 DEGREES
    FORWARD 5 PACES
    TURN LEFT 90 DEGREES
    FORWARD 2 PACES

(b) Write down the least number of instructions that make the pupil walk round the edge of a shape like this.

Figure 4.4

Start at this corner
and go clockwise

(c) Draw the shape the pupil would walk round if these instructions were given.
    REPEAT 3 TIMES [FORWARD 4 PACES; TURN RIGHT 120 DEGREES]

(d) Write down the least number of instructions that make the pupil walk round the edge of a shape like this.

Figure 4.5

Question 3

ECOHEAT sell computer-controlled central heating systems.
One of its engineers installs a computer-controlled central heating system at the Bradford Manufacturing Plc.

(a) Describe how a computer can know the temperature.
(b) Describe what the computer should do if the temperature is too low.
(c) The engineer writes a control program to make the computer keep the temperature at 18°C. Complete the program by writing in line 4.
    Line 1   START
    Line 2   REPEAT LINES 3 TO 5
    Line 3   SET_LEVEL = 18
    Line 4
    Line 5   IF TEMPERATURE IS LESS THAN SET_LEVEL THEN
              TURN HEATER ON
    Line 6   END

(d) Describe how the program would have to be altered if the engineer wanted the central heating system to keep the temperature at 21°C.
(e) Describe one advantage and one disadvantage of a computer-controlled central heating system to Bradford Manufacturing Plc.
(f) Describe one advantage and one disadvantage of a computer-controlled central heating system to Bradford Manufacturing Plc's employees.
(g) Describe one advantage and one disadvantage to Bradford Manufacturing Plc because the engineer works for ECOHEAT.
(h) The computer that controls the central heating system has these design features:
    reliable   CD-ROM drive   speakers
    designer styled hardware   easy to maintain
    Write down the two most important design features.

Question 4

(a) Using words from the list, fill in the table.

| 1 hour | 1 day | 1 week | 10 minutes |
| 1 year | 3 hours | 20 minutes | 10 seconds |

	Time interval for data logging	Period of data logging
To show how temperature changes when water is heated.		
To show how sound levels due to traffic change on a busy main street.		
To show how the number of hours of daylight each day changes throughout the year.		

(b) Remote weather stations are used to collect information about the weather.
  (i) Name three items of information that a remote weather station might collect.
  (ii) Describe how information recorded by a remote weather station could be collected using IT.
  (iii) Describe two uses of information collected from remote weather stations.
  (iv) Describe the advantages and disadvantages of using IT to collect information about the weather.

Question 5

An incubator is used to hatch eggs. The temperature in the incubator has to be kept at a constant temperature or the eggs will not hatch.
(a) Write down the type of sensor that would be used.
(b) Write down the type of actuator that would be used.
(c) Draw a labelled diagram of a computer control system that could be used to control the temperature.
(d) In this context, describe what is meant by feedback.
(e) Describe the possible effects if the incubator becomes too hot or too cold.
(f) Write down one advantage and one disadvantage of using a computer control system.

Question 6

A car park has one entrance, one exit and fifty spaces for cars to park in. The entrance and the exit have automatic barriers to control cars entering and leaving the car park. The car park attendant uses a computer to keep track of the total number of cars in the car park. The computer is connected to the automatic barriers and controls them.

(a) How will the total number of cars in the car park change when the barrier is raised to allow a car:
  (i) Into the car park.
  (ii) To leave the car park.
(b) Describe how the computer can know how many cars there are in the car park.
(c) If the car park is full, the computer will not raise the barrier that controls the entrance. What rule does the computer use in this case?
(d) The car park attendant switches off the computer in the evening before going home. Both barriers are left open so that any cars that are still in the car park can leave. In the morning, the attendant closes the barriers, switches on the computer and runs the computer control system. Later in the day, the attendant discovers that the computer is allowing cars to enter the car park when it is full.

(i) Explain why this happened.
(ii) What should the attendant do in the morning to prevent this happening?
(e) Describe one other reason why the computer might not know the correct number of cars in the car park.

Question 7

(a) Draw a flowchart that describes the operation of a simple fridge.
(b) Write a program in pseudocode that describes how the fridge operates. Identify a conditional statement you have used.
(c) In this context, describe what is meant by feedback.

Question 8

(a) Using words from the list, complete the sentences.

    conditional statement   procedure   circle
    straight line   loop

In a computer program:
  – A .... may change what the program does depending on whether a condition has been satisfied or otherwise.
  – When instructions are repeated over and over this is a ....
  – A self-contained sequence of instructions that can be run from elsewhere in the same program is a ....

(b) In a programming language you are familiar with, give an example of each of the following and explain why you would use it.
(i)   A loop.
(ii) A procedure.
(iii) A conditional statement.

Question 9

A crane is moved around a dockyard. It is controlled by giving a computer instructions.

Example of instructions	What the instructions do
N2	Move the crane North for a distance of 2 units.
W13	Move the crane West for a distance of 13 units.

Figure 4.6

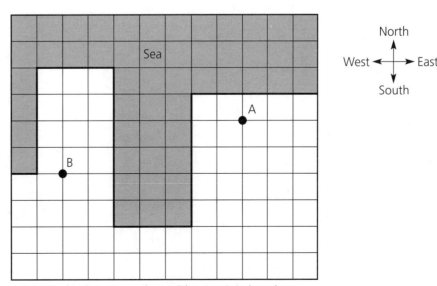

Scale: the squares have sides 1 unit in length

(a) The crane is at point A on the diagram.
    Write the instructions to move the crane from point A to point B.   [2]
(b) A human operator gives the computer the instruction, 4N. Describe how the
    computer should respond.   [2]
(c) The computer can automatically guide the crane around an object in its path.
    – Describe what is needed so that the computer can do this.   [3]
(d) The computer automatically guides the crane around an object.
    (i) In this context describe what is meant by feedback.   [2]
    (ii) Explain why feedback is an essential part of this process.   [2]
(e) The computer can be given new instructions by a human operator when there
    is an object in its path or it can be set up to automatically guide the crane
    around the object.
    – Describe **one** advantage in having a human operator give the computer new
      instructions.
    – Describe **one** advantage in setting up the computer to automatically guide
      the crane around an object.   [2]
                                                                                         SEG

Question 10

John Smith is a Geography teacher whose particular interest has been a study of
local weather conditions. Every day for the last 25 years he has manually collected
data about rainfall, temperature, pressure, sunshine hours, wind speeds and wind
direction. After collecting the data, he has recorded it in an exercise book. When
he has retired he plans to analyse local weather patterns over this 25 year period.

(a) Give **two** problems that can occur by collecting readings in this way.   [2]
(b) An IT teacher has suggested that he uses a computer to help him with this task.
    Name **one** item of software he could buy to help monitor the weather.   [1]
(c) In addition to a computer (which includes a screen, keyboard and mouse):
    (i) Name **two** other items of hardware that he would need to collect the data. [2]
    (ii) Name **two** other items of hardware that he would need to record and
         store the data.   [2]
(d) The temperature and soil moisture of a greenhouse must be controlled and
    must remain between a certain range. The temperature must be kept between
    5 °C and 30 °C and the soil must not get too dry.
       Describe in detail how a computer system and software could be used to
    monitor, control and analyse data from both temperature and soil moisture in the
    greenhouse. In addition to a computer, monitor, hard disk, mouse and printer
    state what other items of hardware could be needed.   [16]
                                                                                         WJEC

5 Applications

REVISION TIPS

Remember what is meant by:

- an application;
- an IT system;
- a manual system;
- on-line;

- interactive;
- multiaccess;
- batch processing;
- real time processing.

Remember the stages of the system's life cycle:

- systems investigation;
- feasibility study;
- system analysis and design;
- program design, coding and testing;

- implementation;
- system documentation;
- evaluation;
- maintenance.

Do not just remember facts. If possible, carefully observe how IT systems are used:

- in schools;
- in supermarkets;
- for banking;
- by the National Lottery;
- for video rental;
- in libraries;

- for booking airline and theatre tickets;
- in estate agents;
- in Tourist Information Centres;
- on motorways for traffic control;
- by road haulage companies;
- for payroll and stock control.

TOPIC OUTLINE

Applications

An **application** is using IT to do a useful task. IT is used throughout commerce and industry for a wide variety of applications. Common commercial applications are payroll; stock control; orders and deliveries; banking; shopping; booking airline tickets; and buying national lottery tickets. Many other applications are referred to elsewhere in this book.

IT systems

- An **IT system** (or Information System) is the whole system of hardware, software and human activities that is used in an application. When an IT system is designed it is important to take into account how human activities and IT will be integrated. To see how important it is that these are integrated effectively you might find it useful to observe carefully what happens when IT systems are used, for example, at supermarket checkouts. IT systems are widely used, for example, for banking (see Figure 5.1 overleaf), libraries, estate agents, Geographic Information Systems (GIS), etc.
- A **legacy** system is an old IT system that is still in use.

Manual systems

- A **manual** system is a system that does not use IT. All the tasks done by the system are done by people or mechanical technologies. In general, manual systems are used before IT systems are installed and are often replaced by them.

Figure 5.1
Using a cashpoint

Processing information

IT systems process information in different ways:

▶ **Interactive** processing takes place when the user and the computer have a 'conversation'. It is a cycle of input, processing, output, and user reaction. Interactive IT systems react to the information input as they are being used. There is an exchange of information between the user and the IT system, for example, the user could provide the IT system with information it needs, modify what it is doing or ask it to do something else.

▶ In an IT system that uses **batch processing**, all the data to be processed is available before processing starts. Data is processed in batches. Batch processing is not interactive. For example, a payroll system can use batch processing.

▶ In an IT system that uses **real time processing**, data is processed as it is input, before any more data is input. Real time systems are very fast and interactive. They are usually run on high-speed, dedicated computers. A **dedicated** computer is only used to run one application. Control applications are often based on dedicated, real time computer systems.

▶ **On-line**, **interactive**, **multiaccess** IT systems are slower than real time systems. Typically they can be accessed by many users over a network and run on general-purpose computers. A **general purpose** computer can be used to run several applications. For example, stock control in a small shop would usually be run on a computer that is used for other tasks, such as wordprocessing and payroll.

The system life cycle

All IT systems are constructed to do some task, are put into practice, are used and then eventually become obsolete. That is, all IT systems go through the stages of the **system life cycle**. These are:

▶ **system investigation** when the task to be done is outlined, and how an IT system could help improve how it is done is briefly described;

▶ **feasibility study** when the proposed IT system is investigated in more detail, and the likely advantages and disadvantages reviewed;

▶ **system analysis and design** when what is required of the IT system is described in detail, and its design is produced;

▶ **program design, coding and testing** when the computer programs or software are created (or generic software is modified) and tested;

▶ **implementation** when the IT system is installed and tested as a whole, and users are trained;

▶ **system documentation** when both user manuals and technical documentation are completed;

▶ **evaluation** when the system is checked to see if it is effectively doing the job it was intended to do;

▶ **maintenance** when errors in the system are corrected and it is extended to meet new requirements.

A **parallel run** (see Figure 5.2) tests the new IT system by running the old system at the same time, and checking that the results produced by both systems are the same. When the new IT system has been thoroughly checked and it is working as it should, the old system is abandoned. The old system could be a manual system or a legacy IT system that is no longer satisfactory.

Figure 5.2
A parallel run

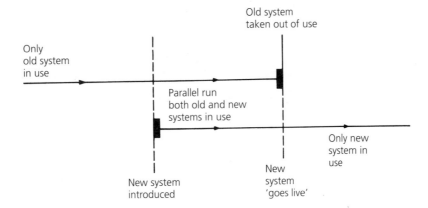

REVISION ACTIVITIES

Question 1

(a) A cheque has printed on it a cheque number.
Ring **one** item to show the input method used.

digital camera	mark sensing	light pen
OCR	MICR	video camera

(b) State **one** item of information printed on the cheque after it has been filled in.

Question 2

(a) Tick **three** boxes to show which applications must use real time processing.

	Tick three boxes
A missile guidance system.	
A supermarket stock control system.	
A computer-controlled robot welder.	
A flight simulator for training pilots.	
Payroll.	
E-mail.	

(b) Using words from the list, complete the sentences.

after   slowly   before   dedicated   quickly   general purpose

– A real time system must process information very ....
– Real time systems usually run on .... computers.
– Information input in a real time system is processed .... any more information is input.

Question 3

(a) A large estate agents thinks it might be a good idea to have an IT system that will let customers see all the houses they have for sale throughout the country.
Using words from the list, complete the sentences.

detective investigation   systems investigation
evaluation   devaluation
implementation   derogation

- To find out how IT could help them, they do a ....
- During the .... of the IT system their staff are trained to use it.
- Every month there is an .... to see if the IT system is still working effectively.

(b) Some customers complain that some of the information about the houses advertised on the IT system is incorrect.
Tick **three** boxes to show why information on an IT system could be incorrect.

	Tick three boxes
The information is correct, it is the customers who are wrong.	
The information provided was inaccurate.	
Mistakes were made when the information was entered into the computer.	
The information has become out-of-date.	
The estate agents have made every effort to make sure the information is accurate.	
The information is not available.	

Question 4

Libraries can use bar codes to control the lending of books to borrowers.

(a) Ring **two** items that would be stored in a bar code on a book.

a description of the book   the purchase price
the book's identity number   a check digit
the number of books in stock   the quantity purchased

(b) Tick **three** boxes to show the advantages in using IT in a library.

	Tick three boxes
The library can print a list of overdue books automatically.	
It is faster to find a book using an on-line library catalogue.	
The library is faster and cheaper.	
Borrowers can get more information about books using an on-line library catalogue.	
Library staff can be paid less as there is less work to do.	
Borrowers are more disconnected if the library is on-line.	

Question 5

A Tourist Information Centre has asked a software company to supply an IT system to deal with bookings for hotel accommodation.

(a) The software company writes the documentation for the IT system. Name two types of documentation and say who would use it.

(b) The software company is also responsible for the maintenance of the IT system. Give two reasons why maintenance might be required.

PRACTICE QUESTIONS

Question 1

Bar codes are printed on the products sold by a supermarket.

(a) Ring **three** items of information that would be stored in a bar code.

colour	number in stock	product code
country of origin	check digit	quantity purchased

(b) Ring **three** items that would be printed on a supermarket receipt.

total to pay	number in stock	share price
bar code	price of goods	quantity purchased

(c) The description of a product can be printed on a supermarket receipt. Describe how this could be done using IT.

(d) Tick **three** boxes to show the advantages in using a supermarket IT system.

	Tick three boxes
Customers are more likely to be charged the correct price.	
The supermarket is cleaner.	
Staff can be paid less as there is widespread unemployment.	
Customers get more information about their purchases.	
Taxis are automatically available for customers as they leave the supermarket.	
The supermarket can change prices faster and more consistently.	

(e) The computer can keep track of the quantity of each product in stock. Describe in detail how this could be done.

(f) The computer can order stock automatically. Describe in detail how this could be done.

(g) Ring **three** items to show the type of processing the supermarket would use.

on-line	interpretative	dedicated
food	interactive	multiaccess

Question 2

A bank gives its customers a plastic bank card that can be used to withdraw money from an Automated Teller Machine (ATM) or cashpoint.

(a) Ring **three** items to show other uses a bank card may have.

evaluation	phone card	cashless payment
MICR	cheque guarantee card	modelling

(b) Ring **one** item to show the technology used to record information on a bank card.

magnetic disk	CD-ROM	OCR
MICR	magnetic stripe	RAM memory

(c) Put these sentences in order to show how a plastic bank card could be used to withdraw money from a cashpoint.

    Select the option that lets you withdraw money.

    Put the plastic card in the slot.

    Wait for the card to be returned, the money to be given out and a receipt to be printed.

    Enter the amount of money.

    Enter your PIN number.

(d) In order to withdraw money from a cashpoint, customers have to know their PIN number.

   (i) Explain what is meant by a PIN number.

   (ii) Explain why a PIN number is used.

(e) Customers can use their bank cards to pay for goods at a supermarket checkout. To do this in France, they would have to enter their PIN number using a key pad connected to the checkout, whereas in the UK, customers are asked to sign a transaction slip.

   Compare and contrast the method used in France and that used in the UK, stating the advantages and disadvantages of each method.

Question 3

A video shop uses an IT system to manage video rentals.

(a) Design a form that would be filled in by new members when they rent a video for the first time.

(b) Members are given a membership card with a bar code on it.

Tick **three** boxes to show why this is done.

	Tick three boxes
It is faster to enter a bar code than type in the member's name.	
A finger print scanner would be faster than a bar code.	
The most popular videos are action movies.	
The least popular videos are documentaries.	
The shop needs to know who has borrowed their videos.	
The membership card identifies the member.	

(c) Each video has a bar code on it.

   (i) Describe what would have to be input to the computer when a member rents several videos.

   (ii) Describe what would have to be input to the computer when the member returns the videos.

   (iii) Give two reasons why your answers to parts (i) and (ii) would be different.

Question 4

The flowchart (see Figure 5.3) shows how a company does payroll processing.

(a) What is the purpose of verification?

(b) Transcription errors can be made when entering data. Describe a common method of verification that might be used to detect a transcription error.

(c) What is the purpose of validation?

(d) A date could be coded in YYMMDD form, for example, 980323 is 23 March 1998.

Figure 5.3

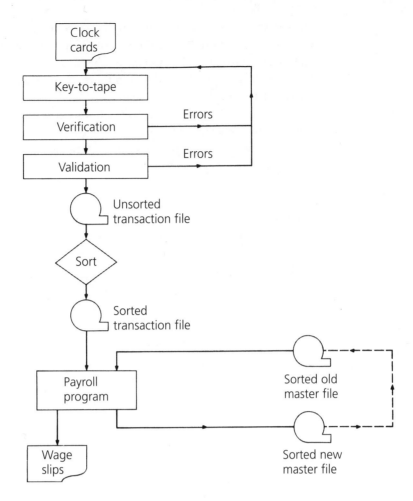

(i) Describe a validation check that might be used to validate the year, that is, YY.

(ii) Explain why legacy IT systems may have a problem processing the year 2000 when dates are coded in this way.

(e) Why would the transaction file be sorted?

(f) The payroll program inputs the clock cards, calculates employees' wages, prints the wage slips and updates the old master file.

(i) Describe what is meant by 'update'.

(ii) Identify three processes that could be carried out when the old master file is updated.

(iii) Describe how an employee's wage could be calculated using the information on the clock cards.

(iv) Draw and label a sketch of an employee's wage slip.

(g) Describe a method of backing up the master file.

(h) Explain why payroll is usually done using batch processing.

Question 5

A sports centre is considering using IT to help with all aspects of organization and administration.

(a) Describe **three** tasks where IT would be useful.

(b) Put these words in order to show the stages in the system's life cycle.

evaluation	implementation
systems investigation	program design, coding and testing
feasibility study	system analysis and design
maintenance	

(c) Using words from the list, complete the sentences.

systems investigation	the holidays
detective investigation	implementation
feasibility study	evaluation

- The sports centre asks a systems analyst to do a .... to find out what IT could be used for and if it could help improve what they do.
- The sports centre asks the systems analyst to do a .... that describes the proposed IT system in more detail, and to review its advantages and disadvantages.
- During .... the new IT system is installed and tested, and the sports centre's staff are trained.

(d) A parallel run of the old manual system and the new IT system should ensure that the new IT system does what it is expected to do. Describe what is meant by a 'parallel run'.

Question 6

The diagram shows a system for processing orders.

Figure 5.4

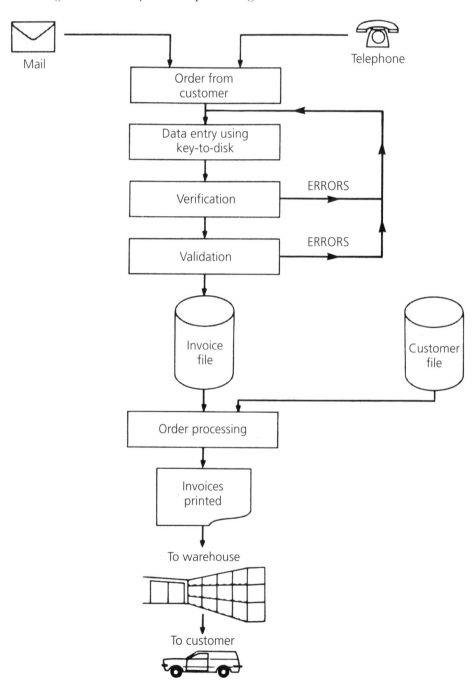

(a) Tick **three** boxes to show why this is a batch processing system.

	Tick three boxes
The orders are processed overnight.	
The orders are processed in batches.	
The invoice file and the customer file are stored on disk.	
Customers can place orders by telephone or by post.	
Order processing is not interactive.	
Printed invoices are sent to the warehouse where the order is assembled and dispatched.	

(b) Using words from the list:

> quantity of each item ordered   customer's name
> customer number   invoice number
> customer's address

  (i) Write down three items of information that would be stored in an order record on the invoice file.

  (ii) Write down three items of information that would be stored in a customer record on the customer file.

(c) Using words from the list, complete the sentences.

> customer file   invoice record
> invoice file   customer number
> customer record

  – The information about a customer that does not change very often is stored in the ....

  – The information about a customer's order is stored in the..............................
    This changes every time an order is placed.

  – Using the .... in an order record, the customer record on the customer file can be found.

(d) Explain why the information on the customer file and the information on the invoice file are stored in two different files.

Question 7

Geographic Information Systems (GIS) can display information on maps.

(a) Tick **three** boxes to show the information that could be usefully displayed by a GIS.

	Tick three boxes
Different road routes from one place to another, showing the cost and time it would take to travel.	
The number and location of burglaries occurring between 11.00 p.m. and 1.00 a.m.	
The total population of the UK.	
The proportion of sales of new cars from each major car manufacturer.	
The location and size of all the secondary schools in an area.	
The chemicals causing pollution in the River Aire.	

(b) Describe a task each of the following could do better using a GIS.
- (i) The police.
- (ii) The ambulance service.
- (iii) A company selling lawn mowers.
- (iv) A supermarket.

(c) A Global Positioning System (GPS) can tell you where you are. Describe two advantages to a road haulage company in using a GPS system combined with a GIS.

(d) A geologist is searching for oil in an unexplored region of South America. Explain why a combined GIS/GPS system might not be very useful to the geologist.

Question 8

A company runs several large theatres. Some of the theatres have flexible areas where the seating can be rearranged for different types of entertainment. Using an on-line booking system, customers can book tickets at the theatres or from ticket agents shops. This diagram shows part of the IT system used.

Figure 5.5

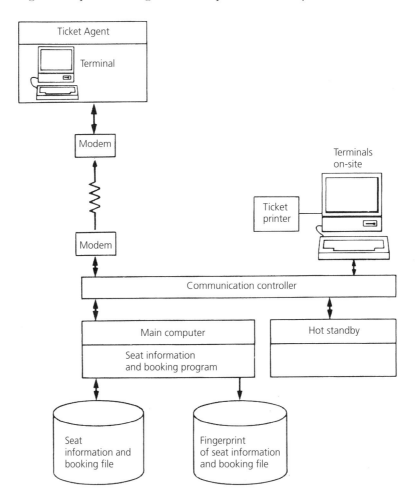

(a) Describe two advantages of the on-line booking system to customers.

(b) Describe two advantages of the on-line booking system to the company.

(c) Describe features of the hardware or software used in an on-line booking system that could help prevent:
- (i) A hacker accessing the IT system, possibly from a ticket agent's shop.
- (ii) The system failing due to the loss of data files.
- (iii) The system failing if the main computer breaks down.

(d) The on-line booking system supports multiaccess and real time processing.
- (i) Explain what is meant by multiaccess.
- (ii) Explain what is meant by real time processing.
- (iii) Explain why multiaccess and real time processing are essential features of an on-line booking system.

Question 9

Members of a library are given a membership card when they join the library. The membership card has a bar code on it.

Figure 5.6

(a) Tick **three** boxes to show which of these statements are true. [3]

	Tick three boxes
The number printed under the bar code is also stored in the bar code.	
Different members have the same number on their membership cards.	
Every member has a different number on their membership card.	
The member's address is stored in the bar code.	
Bar codes can be read into the computer without the need for data preparation.	
The library computer would understand the bar code on a can of baked beans.	

(b) When a member borrows a book, either the bar code on their membership card is read into the computer using a bar code reader, or, the librarian types the number on the card into the computer.
  (i) Explain why a bar code reader is used. [2]
  (ii) Explain why the librarian types in the number. [1]
(c) The bar code has a check digit in it. [1]
  (i) Tick **two** boxes to show which of these statements is true. [2]

	Tick two boxes
When you work out the check digit on a bar code, you should always get the same answer.	
The number under the bar code does not contain the check digit.	
If you know the check digit, you can find out the information stored in the bar code.	
Different bar codes will have the same check digit.	
Every bar code has a different check digit.	

(ii) Check digits can be used to detect errors when a bar code is read.
      Explain how check digits can be used to detect errors.   [2]
(d) Every book in the library has a different bar code in it.

Figure 5.7

(i)   When a member borrows a book from the library, the bar code on their
      membership card and the bar code on the book are read into the computer.
      Explain why **both** bar codes are read.   [2]
(ii) When a member returns a book, only the bar code in the book is read into
      the computer.
      Explain why only the bar code in the book is read.   [2]
(e) The library computer's operating system supports multiaccess and multitasking
     operating methods.
     Explain what is meant by:
     (i)   multitasking;   [1]
     (ii) multiaccess.   [1]

SEG

Question 10
A large firm uses a computer system to handle its payroll operation. The system
uses a master file and a transaction file. These are some of the data items stored:

bank account number	employee address
employee number	hours worked this month
pay rate	tax code
total pay to code	total tax to date

(a) (i)   Name the **one** item which you would expect to be present in both the master
          file and the transaction file.   [1]
    (ii) Explain why this item would have to be in both files.   [1]
    (iii) Choose **four** items which would only be present in the master file.   [4]
(b) How does the system check that the data entered for number of hours worked this
    month is always sensible?   [2]
(c) When the payslips are produced batch processing is used.
    (i)   What type of access to the files is required during batch processing?   [1]
    (ii) Describe the method of backup which would be used to make sure that if
          some of the files were damaged they could be restored.   [2]
(d) The payments to employees are made by transmitting the necessary data to the
    bank. The bank then transfers money into each employee's bank account.
    (i)   The data is encrypted before transmissions. Why is this done?   [1]
    (ii) What data about each employee would have to be transmitted to allow
          payment to be made?   [2]

NEAB

6 IT, hardware, software, operating systems and networks

Remember what is meant by and note the differences between:

- hardware and software;
- mainframes and microcomputers;
- RAM and backing storage;
- LANs and WANs;
- an OS and a NOS.

Remember these input methods, and if possible, observe them in use:

- Optical Mark Recognition (OMR);
- Optical Character Recognition (OCR);
- bar codes;
- Kimball tags;
- Magnetic Ink Character Recognition (MICR);
- magnetic stripe cards;
- voice recognition;
- joystick or tracker ball;
- touch screen;
- sensor.

Remember these output methods, and if possible, observe them in use:

- graph plotter;
- speech synthesis;
- printer;
- actuator.

Remember these security precautions, and if possible, observe them in use:

- backup files;
- User Identification Numbers and Passwords;
- locks, identification cards and guards;
- grills or security laminates;
- clamps and chains;
- loop alarm systems;
- inaccessible network;
- log of users;
- data encryption;
- firewalls;
- virus checks.

TOPIC OUTLINE

Hardware and software

- **Information Technology** is the use of computers and other equipment to store, process and transmit information.
- **Hardware** is the physical equipment, e.g. a monitor.
- **Software** are the programs that control the computer, e.g. a wordprocessor.
- **Mainframes** are large computers.
- **Microcomputers** are Personal Computers (PCs). These can be desk top PCs, portables or laptops. Desk top PCs typically consist of a monitor, a processor box, a hard disk, a floppy disk drive, a keyboard and a mouse. Multimedia PCs (see Figure 6.1) also have a CD-ROM drive and stereo speakers, and may have a microphone, a miniature video camera and a scanner.

Memory
Random Access Memory (RAM) is usually installed in the processor box. Programs and data are stored in RAM while they are being used. RAM is **volatile**, that is, the information stored on it is lost when the computer is switched off.

Backing storage

Backing storage is on hard disk, floppy disk or CD-ROM. Backing storage is **non-volatile**, that is, the information stored on it is not lost when the computer is switched off. The size of memory and backing storage is measured in bytes. A **byte** is the memory required to store 1 character.

> 1 Kilobyte (Kbyte) = 1024 bytes
> 1 Megabyte (Mbyte) = 1024 Kbytes
> 1 Gigabyte (Gbyte) = 1024 Mbytes

▶ Software and data are saved on disk as **files**. A **directory** or **catalogue** is a list of all the files on a disk. Files have a unique **filename** which is given to them when they are created.
▶ **File operations** are:
  − **Saving** a file is copying it from memory to backing storage.
  − **Loading** a file is copying it from backing storage to memory.
  − Two files can be **merged** to form one file.
  − **Updating** a file is editing or amending it to bring it up-to-date.
  − **Deleting** a file is removing it.
  − **Renaming** a file is changing its name.
  − **Copying** a file is making another, identical copy of it.

Figure 6.1
A multimedia PC

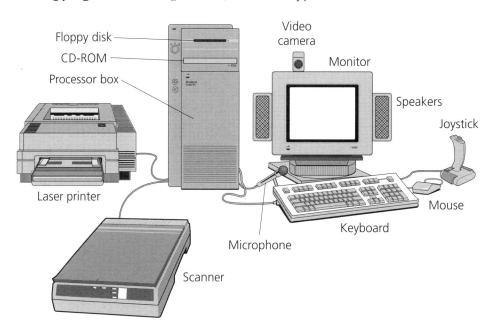

Input

Information can be **input** to a PC using a mouse and a keyboard. Other input methods are:

▶ **Optical Mark Recognition** (OMR), where the position of a mark on a form gives it meaning, e.g. the form used to buy National Lottery tickets (see Figure 2.2).
▶ **Optical Character Recognition** (OCR), where ordinary text is input using a **scanner** and its shape recognized by OCR software. Scanners can also be used to input photographs and drawings.
▶ **Bar codes** can be input using a light pen or laser scanner, e.g. in supermarkets and libraries (see Figure 2.3).
▶ **Kimball tags** (see Figure 6.2) are small punched cards. These are sometimes used by clothes shops.

► **Magnetic Ink Character Recognition** (MICR) (see Figure 6.3) is used to read bank cheques. The characters are printed using magnetic ink and have a distinctive shape.
► **Magnetic stripe cards**, e.g. credit cards (see Figure 2.4).
► A **microphone** can be used to input sound and speech. **Voice recognition** is spoken input. This is a useful input method for disabled people and workers whose hands are occupied, but the number of words recognized can be very limited.

Figure 6.2
A Kimball tag

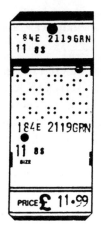

Figure 6.3
A bank cheque uses MICR

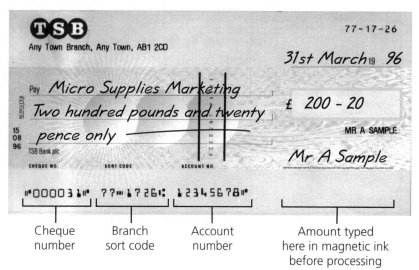

Cheque number   Branch sort code   Account number   Amount typed here in magnetic ink before processing

► **Midi** technology allows sound and music to be input, e.g. from synthesizers and instruments in addition to a microphone.
► A **joystick** or a **tracker ball** can replace a mouse for input to games and GUIs.
► **Touch screens** may be operated using a pen or your finger. They can also be used with GUIs.
► A **video digitizer** can capture single frames or sequences of frames from a video and input them to a computer.
► A **digital camera** takes photographs. These are not recorded on film. The image is recorded in digital form and input directly to the computer.
► **Sensors** are used to record temperature, humidity, light, wind speed, etc.

Output
Information can be **output** from a PC using a monitor, a printer or speakers.

► **Printers** can be:
  – Impact **dot matrix** printers. These are cheap to buy and run. They print slowly and the print quality is poor. Very small impact dot matrix printers are built into supermarket checkouts.
  – **Ink jet** printers. These are cheap to buy but expensive to run. They print slowly but the print quality is very good. These are suitable for the Small Office and Home Office (SoHo).
  – **Laser** printers. These are expensive to buy and run. They print quickly and the print quality is excellent.
► A **printer buffer** is RAM memory built into a printer. It is used to store files while they are waiting to be printed. This releases the computer so that it can continue with other tasks.
► **Spooling** is the queuing of files waiting to be printed on a hard disk. A file is printed when it reaches the front of the queue. Again, this releases the computer so that it can continue with other tasks.
► Other output methods are:
  – **Graph plotters** which can draw high quality designs on large sheets of paper.
  – **Speech synthesis** which is the output of human speech. This is restricted in range and quality but can be useful in situations where reading a screen is difficult.

▶ **Actuators** which are used to perform physical tasks. Actuators can be powered using hydraulics, pneumatics, servo-motors or stepper-motors.

Graphic User Interfaces

A **Graphic User Interface** (GUI) (see Figure 6.4) allows users to operate a computer using Windows, Icons, Menus and Pointers, e.g. Microsoft Windows.

Operating Systems

An **Operating System** (OS) is software that runs between the hardware and the applications software. An OS will:

▶ **Carry out OS commands**. You can give commands through a GUI or type them in on a command line, e.g. COPY C:\ACCESS\DATA\AGENTS A:.

▶ **Supervise programs**. The OS will try to keep programs running whatever difficulties occur. For example, if the OS tries to load a file from a disk and cannot, it does not continue trying or crash, but returns control to you, and explains the problem.

▶ **Make the hardware easy to use**. You do not have to worry about the internal complexities of the computer system.

Figure 6.4
A Graphic
User Interface

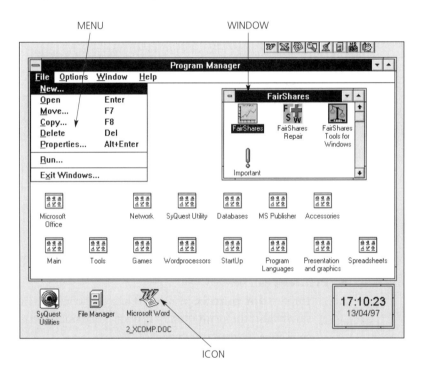

▶ **Help users decide what to do**. For example, if the printer is unavailable when you want to print, it will tell you and ask you what you want to do, perhaps suggesting alternatives.

▶ **Provide utilities to manage the computer system**. For example, to format floppy disks.

▶ **Optimize the use of the computer's resources**. For example, so that printing can be done while you are doing other tasks on the computer.

▶ **Support multitasking**, that is, running more than one piece of software on the same computer at the same time. For example, you could run a wordprocessor in one window and graphics software in another.

▶ **Make programs portable**, so that they can be run on different computers with the same OS.

Networks

A **network** allows users to share software and hardware, and communicate with other networks. A **Local Area Network** (LAN) (see Figure 6.5) is a small network, probably in one room or a building. A **Wide Area Network** (WAN) is a widespread network, probably national or international. Computers can be directly connected to a LAN, but will probably connect to a WAN using a modem and the telephone network.

Network Operating Systems

A **Network Operating System** (NOS) is an OS that can:

▶ **Allow networked computers to communicate**, e.g. using e-mail.
▶ **Support multiaccess**, that is, where more than one person accesses the same computer at the same time.
▶ **Allow users to share software and data stored on a fileserver**. For example, a wordprocessor stored on a fileserver can be used from any network station.
▶ **Allow users to share hardware**. For example, networked printers.

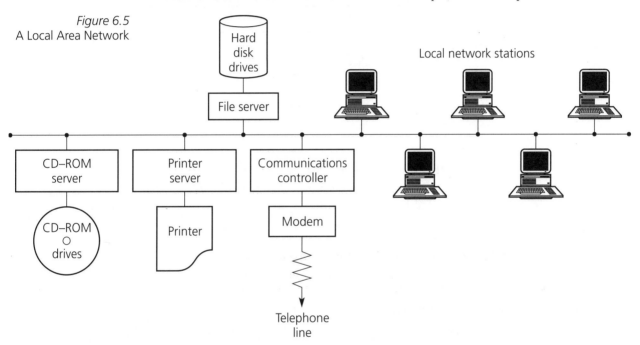

Figure 6.5
A Local Area Network

▶ **Manage printer queues and spooling**. When a file is sent to a network printer, the NOS puts it in the printer queue on the fileserver, and prints it when it gets to the front of the queue.
▶ **Organize User Identification Numbers and Passwords**.
▶ **Keep a log of who uses the network**.

Security

The **security** of IT systems is important to protect users' investments in software and hardware. To help keep IT systems secure, users should:

▶ backup files regularly, using the ancestral system;
▶ limit access to IT systems using User Identification Numbers and Passwords, and change passwords frequently;
▶ use locks, identification cards and guards to control access to IT rooms;
▶ put grills or security laminates on the windows of IT rooms;
▶ attach computers to desks or walls using clamps and chains;

▶ use loop alarm systems that are always active on all computers, in addition to other alarm systems;

▶ install the network cable where it is inaccessible;

▶ keep a log of users;

▶ use data encryption techniques to encode all data on networks;

▶ use firewalls to prevent access from external networks;

▶ use automatic virus checks.

REVISION ACTIVITIES

Question 1

(a) Fill in the table to show what is hardware and what is software.

	Write down 'hardware' or 'software'
A monitor.	
A wordprocessor.	
A printer.	
A mouse.	
A database.	
A modem.	

(b) Ring **three** items that are part of a desk top PC.

gateway	mainframe	non-volatile	keyboard
hard disk	monitor	heat sensor	hydraulic motor

Question 2

(a) Using words from the list, complete these sentences.

2.4 Gbyte	processor box
a CD-ROM drive	32 Mbyte
microprocessor	stereo speakers

– Multimedia computers are similar to ordinary desk top PCs but they also have .... and ....

– A desk top computer could have a .... RAM memory and a .... hard disk.

– RAM memory and a hard disk are usually built into the ....

(b) Fill in the table to show which hardware devices are used for input or output.

	Write down 'input' or 'output'
A monitor.	
Keyboard.	
Speaker.	
A mouse.	
Scanner.	
A printer.	

Question 3

(a) Ring **three** items to show which of the following are used as backing storage.

     megabyte   hard disk   floppy disk   CD-ROM   memory   fax

(b) Using words from the list, complete the sentences.

     save   merge   copy   delete   update

   – When you .... a file it is copied from memory to backing storage.
   – When you .... a file on a floppy disk it is removed from it.
   – When you .... a file it is edited to bring it up-to-date.

Question 4

(a) Using words from the list, complete the sentences.

     OMR   Bar codes   MICR   OCR   Kimball tags

   – The form used to buy National Lottery tickets uses ....
   – .... can be used in libraries to identify books.
   – .... is used on bank cheques. The characters are printed using magnetic ink and have a distinctive shape.

(b) Tick **three** boxes to show which of the following statements are true.

	Tick three boxes
Information can be output from a PC using a monitor, a printer or speakers.	
A printer buffer is RAM memory built into a printer.	
Graph plotters are used to output high quality line drawings on large sheets of paper.	
Spooling is a form of macramé.	
OMR produces better quality video than VCR.	
Speech synthesis is using human speech to control a computer.	

Question 5

(a) Ring **three** items to show the tasks done by an Operating System.

    supervise programs   select a font   support multitasking
    format a paragraph   do a spelling check   format a floppy disk

(b) Tick **three** boxes to show which of the following would help keep an IT system secure.

	Tick three boxes
Leave computer rooms open in the evening so that the cleaners can get in.	
Ignore virus checks as these are no longer a problem.	
Backup files regularly.	
Use firewalls to prevent access from external networks.	
Switch off all alarm systems during the day.	
Use User Identification Numbers and Passwords.	

PRACTICE QUESTIONS

Question 1

(a) Tick **three** boxes to show which of the following statements are true.

	Tick three boxes
A database is computer software.	
Desk top PCs, portables and laptops are examples of mainframe computers.	
A printer is a hardware device.	
A mainframe is part of the processor box on a PC.	
Information Technology is the use of computers and other equipment to store, process and transmit information.	
A modem is computer software.	

(b) Using words from the list, complete the sentences.

archives   backing storage
a desk top PC   Random Access Memory
cyberspace   megabytes

– A keyboard, mouse, monitor, processor box, hard disk and floppy disk drive are part of ....
– The information stored in .... is lost when the computer is switched off.
– The information stored on .... is not lost when the computer is switched off.
– Examples of .... are a hard disk and a CD-ROM.

(c) Explain what is meant by each of the following:
  (i)   A file.   (iv) Renaming a file.
  (ii) A directory.   (v) Copying a file.
  (iii) Loading a file.   (vi) Merging two files.

Question 2

(a) Name three hardware devices that can be used to input information to a desk top PC.
(b) Name three hardware devices that can be used to output information from a desk top PC.
(c) Describe an example of the use of each of the following input methods.
  (i)   Joystick.   (v)   Magnetic stripe cards.
  (ii) OMR.   (vi) Bar codes.
  (iii) OCR.   (vii) Touch screen.
  (iv) Kimball tags.
(d) Magnetic Ink Character Recognition (MICR) is used to read bank cheques.
  (i)   Draw a labelled diagram of a bank cheque.
  (ii) Name those items of information on a cheque that can be input to a computer using MICR.
  (iii) After the cheque has been filled in, the bank types a further item of information onto the cheque. This item can be read using MICR. Name this item of information.

Question 3

(a) Describe what is meant by voice recognition. Name a suitable input device.

(b) Describe one situation in which voice recognition could be a useful means of controlling a computer.

(c) Describe what is meant by speech synthesis. Name a suitable output device.

(d) Describe one situation in which speech synthesis could be a useful output method.

(e) Midi technology allows sound and music to be manipulated by a computer. Describe how this could affect the ways in which recorded music is produced.

Question 4

(a) Name one type of software that could be used to produce a school newspaper.

(b) Describe three features of the software you have chosen that make it suitable for producing a school newspaper.

(c) A photograph of the school is to be included in the school newspaper. Using words from the list, describe how this could be done.

    cut and paste   edit

    scanner   input

    format

  – The photograph is placed in the ....

  – The photograph is .... to the computer.

  – Using graphics software, you can .... the photograph.

  – The photograph is imported into the software being used to produce the school newspaper using ....

(d) Ring **three** other sources of photographs and illustrations for including in a newspaper.

    video digitizer   dot matrix printer   monitor

    sensor   digital camera   clip art library

(e) Ring **three** sources of text for including in a newspaper.

    wordprocessing document   clip art library   processor

    OCR scanning   monitor   e-mail message

Question 5

(a) Tick **three** boxes to show which of the following statements are true.

	Tick three boxes
Colour printing is faster than black-and-white printing.	
Spooling is the queuing of files waiting to be printed on a hard disk.	
Using printer buffers or spooling releases the computer so that it can continue with other tasks.	
Using a hard disk will slow down printing.	
A printer buffer is RAM memory built into a printer.	
Using a floppy disk will speed up printing.	

(b) Give **two** reasons why a small impact dot matrix printer is most suitable for producing credit card transaction slips.

Question 6

(a) A Graphic User Interface (GUI) allows users to operate a computer using Windows, Icons, Menus and Pointers. In this context, using a diagram or otherwise, explain what is meant by:

(i) A window.

(ii) An icon.

(iii) A menu.

(iv) A pointer.

(b) Give two reasons why most computer users prefer using a GUI to typing in text OS commands.

(c) Using words from the list, complete the sentences.

multiplication	sharing
multitasking	common sense
division	multiaccess

– A Network Operating System allows the .... of software and data stored on a fileserver.

– Using .... more than one person can access the same computer at the same time.

– Using .... you could run a database in one window and graphics software in another.

(d) Describe three other tasks that can be done by a Network Operating System.

Question 7

(a) Tick **three** boxes to show which of the following statements are true.

	Tick three boxes
A Local Area Network (LAN) is a small network, probably in one room or a building.	
A browser is a large, docile sheep.	
The Internet is controlled by robocops who operate in cyberspace.	
The Internet is an international network made up of smaller, interconnected networks.	
Virtual reality is just like wandering around in the garden.	
A Wide Area Network (WAN) is a national or international network.	

(b) Describe three different types of information available on the WWW.

Question 8

A school has a network of computers for use by teachers and pupils.

(a) Draw a diagram of the network showing the links between the hardware devices connected to it.

(b) Explain what is meant by:

(i) A fileserver.

(ii) A LAN.

(iii) A WAN.

(c) When pupils use a computer attached to the network, they can save their work on either the fileserver or on their own floppy disk.

(i)   State one advantage to pupils if they save their work on their own floppy disks.

(ii) State one advantage to the network manager if pupils save their work on their own floppy disks.

(iii) State one advantage to pupils if they save their work on the fileserver.

(iv) State one advantage to the network manager if pupils save their work on the fileserver.

(d) Pupils print draft copies of their work on an impact dot matrix printer. They then check the draft copy for mistakes. If there are no mistakes pupils print the final copy on a laser printer.

(i)   State one advantage and one disadvantage in using a dot matrix printer to print draft copies.

(ii) State one advantage and one disadvantage in using a laser printer to print the final copy.

(e) Describe two security problems when a network is used in a school. Describe a method of overcoming each security problem.

Question 9

An office worker uses this computer.

Figure 6.6

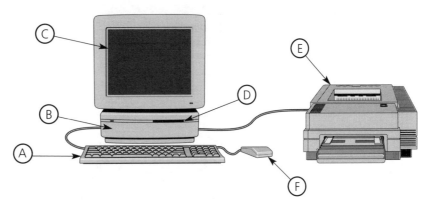

(a) (i)   The office worker needs to know the names of the different parts of the computer. Write down the label of the part next to its name.   [1]

Name of part	Label
keyboard	
monitor	
printer	

(ii) Write down the labels of the parts used to input information into the computer. [2]

(iii) Write down the labels of the parts used to output information from the computer.   [2]

(b) The computer is connected to a Local Area Network using a network card. The network card is installed inside a part of the computer. Write down a label of the part that contains the network card.   [1]

(c) When the computer is switched on, the office worker has to enter a password.

(i)   Explain why passwords are used.   [1]

(ii) The office worker's password has to be changed every week. Explain why passwords should be changed regularly.   [1]

(iii) When the password was changed, the office worker typed in the new password. The password was typed in correctly. The computer asked the office worker to type in the new password again. Explain why the computer asked the office worker to type in the new password again.   [1]

(d) The office worker wants to access information on a computer in Australia. This is part of a flowchart that shows what the office worker has to do to access the information.

Figure 6.7

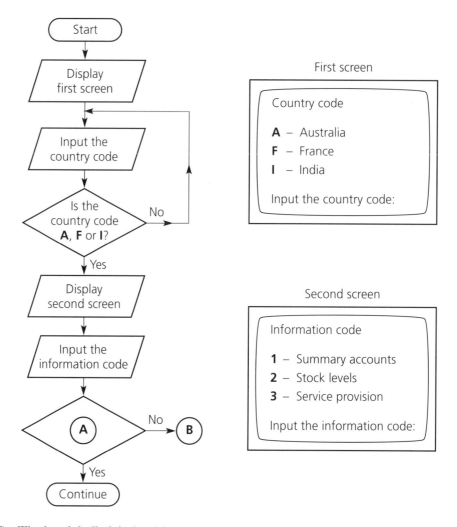

First screen

Country code

A – Australia
F – France
I – India

Input the country code:

Second screen

Information code

1 – Summary accounts
2 – Stock levels
3 – Service provision

Input the information code:

(i)   The box labelled **A** should contain a question.
      Write down the question that should be in the box labelled A.   [2]
(ii) The line labelled **B** should re-join the flowchart.
      Draw on the flowchart to show where the line labelled B should re-join the
      flowchart.   [1]
                                                                                                      SEG

Question 10
A sports shop has recently bought a multimedia computer system.

(a) What is meant by multimedia?   [1]
(b) A supplier of sports equipment usually advertises in a catalogue which is sent to
    customers' homes and local sports shops. Recently it has expanded its stock and
    can only advertise a few of its range of items in the catalogue. The company is
    investigating using CD-ROM disks to store its catalogue of goods for sale.
    (i)   Describe how customers could access the catalogue data stored on the disk.   [2]
    (ii) Give **one** advantage to the customer and **one** advantage to the sports firm
          in storing the catalogue data on a CD-ROM disk rather than in the form of a
          printed catalogue.   [2]
(c) The sports shop can use its multimedia computer to run the sports equipment
    catalogue CD-ROM disks sent by the sports equipment suppliers.
    Give **one** example of how the multimedia facilities of the computer system can
    be used to give information to customers.   [1]
                                                                                                     WJEC

Social implications

REVISION TIPS

Observe and remember the effects of IT on:

- lifestyle;
- employment;
- privacy;
- freedom.

Find out how to program and use:

- a radio alarm clock;
- a washing machine;
- a video recorder;
- central heating controls;
- security alarm and lighting controls;
- a dish washer.

Contact those institutions that store your personal information using IT, and ask them for a copy of it. Check it and ask them to correct it if necessary. These could include your:

- school;
- church;
- bank;
- building society;
- sports club;
- youth club.

Observe and remember, how and why:

- CCTV is used;
- stripe card operated entry control and registration systems are used.

TOPIC OUTLINE

Lifestyle

Lifestyle and leisure are affected by developments in IT.

- **Domestic work** has been made easier, for example, automatic washing machines have replaced manual washers. Such developments have made it easier for people to take part in education, employment and social activities outside the home.
- **Home entertainment** and the other ways we spend our leisure time are enriched by the technology we have access to at home. For example, broadcast, cable and satellite TV; teletext, home computers with multimedia for work, education and games; programmable video recorders; and Internet access.
- **Personal communications** can be extended using mobile telephones, the WWW and the Internet. For example, e-mail can be available at work and at home, and in other locations using a mobile telephone.
- **On-line shopping and banking** are both possible from home. Users can select from a vast range of goods available in virtual shopping centres throughout the world. On-line banking allows users to buy and sell shares, and transfer money between accounts instantly. Such services may be available by direct on-line connection or using the WWW.
- **Cash-less society**: magnetic stripe cards, for example bank cards and credit cards, have led to a dramatic reduction in the use of cash in notes and coins. Users can

obtain money and bank statements, or deposit cheques, etc. all day, every day. Foreign currency can be obtained from cashpoints in many countries overseas. This has reduced the need for over-the-counter services in banks. As a result the number of bank branches has declined and telephone banking has become increasingly popular.

Employment

As IT is introduced into the workplace a number of changes take place.

▶ Some jobs disappear and some skills are no longer needed. For example, there are now very few watchmakers who can build and repair mechanical watches but many electronic digital watches are made. Automatic telephone exchanges give faster connection without the need to employ large numbers of switchboard operators.

▶ Some jobs are done in new ways. For example, typists have been replaced by wordprocessor operators.

▶ New jobs are created. For example, manufacturing hardware and writing software.

▶ New ways of organizing work arise. For example, teleworking where workers work from home using IT to communicate with colleagues. Teleworking helps the house-bound find work; improves the environment by reducing traffic congestion; and cuts employers' expenses by reducing the costs of a central workplace.

Privacy

IT systems can store very large volumes of information and give fast access to it. Personal information about you and your family may be stored by doctors and hospitals, the DHSS, local authorities, schools, the police, banks, employers and others. These systems can improve the quality of services but your privacy may suffer.

The **Data Protection Act** (1984) regulates the use of personal information. Users of personal information must register with the Data Protection Registrar, and they must comply with the principles of good practice, which state that information must be:

▶ obtained fairly and by lawful means;

▶ held and used only for authorized purposes;

▶ disclosed only to authorized people;

▶ relevant to its registered use;

▶ adequate in scope for the use to which it will be put but not excessive;

▶ accurate and up-to-date;

▶ held no longer than is needed for its registered use;

▶ accessible to the individuals whose personal information is stored; on request, they should be told what personal information is kept about them, and allowed to correct it if necessary;

▶ confidential and secure.

Freedom

IT can help track individuals and match this with other information about them. This could affect their freedom of movement and association.

▶ **Entry control systems** using stripe cards now regulate access to many institutions, including schools and FE colleges, and can control access to areas within buildings such as IT rooms. These systems can track an individual's presence within the institution, even on multiple sites. Such systems could be developed so that an individual's presence is recorded automatically as they move around a building.

▶ **Electronic tagging** of criminals has been used to limit their freedom of movement. The movements of an individual fitted with an electronic tag can be monitored, and action taken if the individual moves outside the limits of, for example, their home.

▶ **Transport control** IT systems can identify cars that are speeding and fine their owners automatically. In the future, these could also automatically charge motorists for using motorways. Such systems could track cars as they enter and leave motorways, and provide information about their movements throughout the national and international road network.

▶ **Closed Circuit Television** (CCTV) cameras record much of what happens in town centres (see Figure 7.1). In the future, IT systems might automatically identify individuals using town centres and other areas.

▶ **Telecommunications** by fax, e-mail and telephone can be automatically monitored, recorded and de-coded by the network providers working with the police and security services.

IT systems that track individuals' movements and monitor their activities have many beneficial uses. They help prevent unauthorized access to buildings and other areas so that those who intend mischief or vandalism are constrained or more easily caught. They can help prevent antisocial and criminal behaviour, and assist the police in detecting and arresting criminals and terrorists. However, the same IT systems that can protect individuals' freedom of movement and association could also be used to enforce unreasonable levels of social control.

Figure 7.1
CCTV in use

REVISION ACTIVITIES

Question 1

(a) Tick **three** boxes to show which of the following statements are true.

	Tick three boxes
Computer programmers and systems analysts are in great demand as companies install IT systems.	
Computer-controlled robot welding machines are less accurate than human welders.	
There are fewer watchmakers who can build and repair mechanical watches.	
Checkout operators do not need quick, accurate mental arithmetic as automatic tills can add up customers' bills and calculate the change required faster and more accurately.	
Calculators have become larger and more unwieldy as microprocessor technology has been built into them.	
Automatic stock control and ordering has led to an increase in the numbers employed in retail sales.	

(b) Ring **three** jobs where IT has dramatically changed the skills required to do them.

    secretary   bricklayer   plumber

    policeman   bank clerk   cleaner

Question 2

(a) Using words from the list, complete these sentences.

    stored   illuminated   disproved

    described   improved   searched

   – Information stored in large databases can be .... quickly and accurately.

   – IT systems have .... the quality of services but privacy may suffer.

(b) Tick **three** boxes to show which of the following comply with the Data Protection Act (1984).

	Tick three boxes
When collecting information, you should collect as much as possible in case it is needed later.	
Personal information must be kept accurate and up-to-date.	
Anyone can use personal information stored on a computer.	
Anyone who asks must be told what information is kept about them, and allowed to change it if it is incorrect.	
Personal information should only be kept as long as it is needed.	
To make sure that personal information is correct you should print it all out and display it on a public notice board.	

Question 3

(a) Ring **three** methods that can be used to track individuals' movements.

video-on-demand   MICR   CCTV

stripe cards   video conferencing   electronic tag

(b) Tick **three** boxes to show which of the following are true.

	Tick three boxes
Stripe card operated entrances could register pupils and prevent unauthorized people getting into schools.	
IT systems on motorways can identify cars that are speeding and fine their owners automatically.	
IT systems that track individuals' movements could not be used to enforce unreasonable levels of social control.	
IT systems that track individuals' movements do not help prevent antisocial and criminal behaviour.	
CCTV cameras are switched off in the evenings.	
Criminals can have electronic tags fitted so that if they move outside their homes the police are informed.	

Question 4

(a) Ring **three** programmable systems.

radio   TV   iron

security alarm system   video recorder   washing machine

(b) Write '**true**' or '**false**' next to each of the following statements.

	Write 'true' or 'false'
Older washing machines had hand-operated agitators and wringers. In a modern machine these are automatically controlled by a built-in program.	
It is more convenient to go to the nearest bank during opening hours than to use telephone banking from home.	
You can only purchase virtual goods in a virtual shopping mall.	
Cable companies provide TV, and offer a range of other services, including telephone and Internet access.	
Access to e-mail from home is useful for teleworkers.	
Using a bank card, you can obtain foreign currency from cashpoints in Europe.	

Question 5

(a) Using words from the list, complete these sentences.

relaxed   down sized   teleworking

confusing   regulated   essential

– Knowledge of IT is increasingly .... for all workers.

- Working from home using IT to communicate with employers and customers is called ....
- The use of personal information stored on computers is .... by the Data Protection Act.

(b) Ring **three** developments that make it easier for many people to work from home.

    motorways   e-mail   TVs

    fibre optic cables   pylons   cheap PCs

? PRACTICE QUESTIONS

Question 1

A family is considering purchasing a home computer. The computer will be used for work and for leisure activities.

(a) Ring the **three** features of a home computer that would make it most suitable for work.

    games software   industry standard software   laser printer

    e-mail connection   speakers   dot matrix printer

(b) Ring the **three** features of a home computer that would make it most suitable for leisure use.

    wordprocessing software   security fixings   joystick

    speakers   CD-ROM   thermostat

(c) Using a labelled diagram, describe a multimedia home computer system.

(d) State one advantage and one disadvantage of teleworking.

Question 2

A school uses IT to handle personal information about pupils.

(a) Tick **three** boxes to show which items of personal information about pupils the school would store.

	Tick three boxes
Name.	
Favourite food.	
Emergency telephone number.	
Doctor.	
Height.	
Bank balance.	

(b) Name four other items of personal information about each pupil you would expect the school to store.

(c) Tick **three** boxes to show the different ways the school could check that pupils' personal information is accurate and which comply with the requirements of the Data Protection Act.

	Tick three boxes
Give pupils a copy of their own personal information and ask them to check it.	
Print out all the information about all the pupils in a form, and pin it on the form's notice board.	
Publish the information in the school newspaper and ask anyone who thinks it is incorrect to see the school secretary.	
Send parents a copy of the personal information about their children that the school has recorded and ask them to check it.	
Ask a teacher to interview pupils in private and check that what has been stored is correct.	
Wait until a parent or pupil complains.	

(d) The school stores pupils' personal information on a network that is used by office staff, teachers and pupils. Describe two security problems that could arise and explain how you would try to prevent each of them.

Question 3
(a) IT systems can identify cars that are speeding and fine their owners automatically.
  (i)   Describe how this could be done.
  (ii) Describe one possible advantage to drivers.
  (iii) Describe one possible disadvantage to drivers.
(b) It is proposed to charge drivers for using motorways.
  (i)   Describe how this could be done automatically using an IT system.
  (ii) Describe one possible advantage to drivers.
  (iii) Describe one possible disadvantage to drivers.
(c) Drivers can buy petrol using credit cards and other magnetic stripe cards.
  (i)   Describe one advantage to petrol stations.
  (ii) Describe one possible advantage to drivers.
  (iii) Describe one possible disadvantage to drivers.
(d) Interconnected IT systems for speed control, motorway charging and credit cards could be used to track motorists' routes.
  (i)   Describe one advantage to drivers.
  (ii) Describe one disadvantage to drivers.

Question 4
(a) Access to the Internet and the WWW is now available from home.
  (i)   Describe what is needed for access to the WWW from home.
  (ii) Describe two types of information you would expect to find on the WWW.
  (iii) Describe two ways of finding the information you want on the WWW.
(b) On-line shopping from home could help disabled people and others who are housebound.
  (i)   Describe what is meant by on-line shopping.
  (ii) State two advantages to a customer of on-line shopping compared with a visit to the local shops.
  (iii) State two disadvantages to a customer of on-line shopping compared with a visit to the local shops.
(c) On-line banking is increasingly popular.
  (i)   Describe two tasks that you would expect to be able to do on connection to an on-line bank.
  (ii) State two advantages to a customer of on-line banking.
  (iii) State two disadvantages to a customer of on-line banking.

(d) The information on the WWW is not regulated by a central organization.
  (i)   Describe two types of information on the WWW that parents and teachers might consider to be undesirable.
  (ii) Explain why parents and teachers might be concerned about this lack of regulation.
  (iii) Describe how the information available can be censored.

Question 5

In 1980, fewer people had bank accounts and the use of stripe card technology in banking information systems was just being introduced in some areas. You had to go to a branch of your bank in order to withdraw cash.

(a) State one facility now available to banks' customers that depends on IT.
(b) State one advantage and one disadvantage to the banks' customers due to its use of IT.
(c) State one way the use of IT in banking has changed the job of a bank clerk.
(d) State one way the banks' use of IT has changed the job of a shop assistant.
(e) State one advantage of the 'cashless society' to a shop owner.

Question 6

(a) Describe the impact the use of IT at work has had on:
  (i)   The number of jobs available.
  (ii) The skills needed to find a job.
  (iii) The exposure of employees to dirty and dangerous working conditions.
  (iv) The productivity of workers.
(b) Robots are often used to manufacture cars.
  (i)   Describe two situations where it would be better to use robots than people.
  (ii) Describe two situations where it would be better to use people than robots.
(c) It is expected that the use of IT in offices will lead to the 'paper-less office'.
    Ring **three** developments that could lead to the 'paper-less office'.
       laser printing   file sharing   fax
       DTP   e-mail   networks
(d) It is thought that IT may polarize society into those who have access to IT resources and those who do not. Describe the impact this would have on the lives of the 'haves' and the 'have nots'.

Question 7

Electronic tagging can be used to track individuals.

(a) Describe how electronic tagging could be used to restrict individuals to their homes.
(b) Give two reasons why this might not be successful.
(c) Describe one situation in which this could be of benefit to society.
(d) Describe one situation where this might not be acceptable to society.

Question 8

(a) It is sometimes said that IT is creating a 'global village'. Explain what is meant by this, and describe the developments that have led to it.
(b) The labour market is increasingly international and workers in the UK have to compete for jobs with workers in other countries. Describe how IT has contributed to the internationalization of the labour market, and how it can help attract jobs to the UK.
(c) In this context, explain why it is important that different types of computer should be able to exchange information and communicate with each other.
(d) In this context, give a reasoned argument for and against the participation of the UK in the European Community.

Question 9

Total for this question: 9 marks

A bank holds personal information about its customers on a computer file.

(a) Write down **one** item of personal information about a customer other than the customer's name, address and customer number. [1]

(b) Complete these sentences, using terms from the list. [2]

    direct   file   open

    field   key   sequential

A customer's name is a .... within a customer's record.

Each customer has a unique customer number. This is used as a

.... field.

(c) The bank stores all customers' personal information on a computer at its Head Office in Swindon. The bank allows its branches throughout the country to access this information.

Tick **two** boxes to show which of these statements are true. [2]

	Tick two boxes
A Local Area Network is used to work out how many rooms there should be within a branch of the bank.	
A Local Area Network connects the computers within a branch of the bank.	
A Graphic User Interface is a global computer network.	
Electronic mail is used by the factory that makes computers to send them to customers.	
A Wide Area Network connects the computers at a branch of the bank to the computer in Swindon.	

(d) The bank allows customers to withdraw money from its network of Automated Teller Machines (ATMs). ATMs are also known as 'cashpoints' or 'holes in the wall'.

(i) Describe how a customer withdraws money from an ATM. [2]

(ii) Describe how the introduction of ATMs has changed the lifestyle of customers. [2]

SEG

Question 10

Mail order companies store personal data about their customers on computer files. The Data Protection Act is designed to protect customers from data misuse.

(a) Give **three** rights that this Act gives to the customer. [3]

(b) Accidental damage to, or loss of, data has to be prevented. Describe **three** precautions that data users should take to try to stop this from happening. [3]

NEAB

Solutions
Communicating information

1

SOLUTIONS TO REVISION ACTIVITIES

Question 1
- You can load and save files using wordprocessing, DTP and graphics software.
- You can communicate very quickly over long distances using e-mail.
- Using video conferencing, you can see and talk to people in other countries.

Question 2
Brush size adjustment; freehand drawing tool; colour palette; zoom in and out; block copy, cut and paste; enlargement; box drawing tool.

Question 3
(a) Paragraph; font.
(b) Italics; bold; underline; strikethrough; capitals.

Question 4
(a) Load or open a file; import clip art; use a different font; save or close a file; re-size clip art; print; use a different text size.
(b) – Layout text and graphics in columns.
   - Edit an article that has been imported from a wordprocessor.
   - Import a picture taken using a digital camera.

Question 5
(a) Teacher; doctor; security alarm company; student; textile designer.
(b) Any reasonable answer, for example: better quality presentation, including different text fonts and sizes, and clip art; spelling checks can be done automatically; can draft and re-draft without making the work messy.

SOLUTIONS TO PRACTICE QUESTIONS

Question 1
(a) – Different text styles and fonts can be used in a wordprocessing document.
   - You can make several printed copies of a document prepared using a wordprocessor.
   - If you do not save your work, when you switch off the computer it will be lost.
(b) DTP; e-mail; wordprocessing.

Question 2
(a) Any reasonable answer, for example: Microsoft Word
(b) Any reasonable answer, for example: a desk top PC, including mouse, keyboard, monitor, processor box with a hard disk and a floppy disk drive, and a printer.
(c) (i) Any reasonable answer, for example: in the file menu select open; select the drive, directory and filename, click on OK.
   (ii) Any reasonable answer, for example: highlight the text; in the format menu select the text size required, click on OK.
   (iii) Any reasonable answer, for example: highlight the text; drag the highlighted text to its new position.

(iv) Any reasonable answer, for example: in the tools menu, select spelling; when prompted change or ignore incorrect spellings.

(v) Any reasonable answer, for example: press the print button on the tool bar.

(vi) Any reasonable answer, for example: press the save button on the tool bar.

Question 3

(a) Any reasonable answer, for example: highlight the diagram; in the edit menu select cut; move the cursor to the new position; in the edit menu select paste.

(b) Any reasonable answer, for example: the science teacher may want the worksheet displayed at 100 per cent magnification while editing it but display the whole page on the screen to see if the page layout is acceptable.

(c) – Any printer that produces a good quality image, for example, a laser printer or an ink jet printer.

    – Any reasonable answer, for example: a good quality image is needed as the science teacher will want to photocopy the worksheet.

Question 4

(a) Any reasonable answer, for example: *Hardware*: a desk top PC with a mouse, keyboard, monitor, processor box with a hard disk and a floppy disk drive, and a printer. *Software*: an Operating System and a wordprocessor.

(b) Any reasonable answer, for example: assuming the picture is a photograph: *Hardware*: in addition to a desk top PC a scanner is needed. *Software*: scanning software. *How this is done*: place the photograph face down in the scanner; in the file menu select acquire; preview the scan adjusting the quality and area to be scanned, select scan.

(c) Any reasonable answer, for example: in a mail merge, a database of customers' personal information is merged with a standard letter to produce a personalized letter to be sent to each customer. To do mail merge you would: set up a database of customers' names and addresses and other personal information; write a standard letter that includes merge fields where customers' personal information is to be inserted; run the mail merge.

Question 5

(a) Any reasonable answer, for example: as the engineers move around, working on jobs for different clients they find it time-consuming to keep in direct contact with the company by telephone. E-mail could improve communications as the company and its engineers do not have to be in direct contact by telephone. They can contact each other when this is convenient. In addition, technical documents and diagrams can be transferred by e-mail.

(b) A diagram showing at least: the engineer's PC and modem linked to the telephone network; the company's PC and modem linked to the telephone network.

(c) Any reasonable answer, for example: using e-mail software, write the message and attach any required documents to it; in the file menu, select send.

(d) Any reasonable answer, for example: *Advantage*: it is quicker to distribute the same e-mail message to all the company's engineers than to contact each of them by telephone. *Disadvantage*: engineers may not get messages when the company wants them to as they do not look at their e-mail often enough.

(e) Any reasonable answer, for example: *Advantage*: e-mail messages can be inspected at the company's and the engineer's convenience so possible time differences are less important; detailed technical documents can be transferred faster and more securely. *Disadvantage*: the engineer may not have easy access to a reliable telephone network.

Question 6

(a) Any reasonable poster showing at least: the name of the clothes shop and its logo; where and when the sale is; the reductions on jeans and socks; some relevant illustrations; large size text has been used.

(b) Desk top publishing software, e.g. Microsoft® Publisher, or graphics software, e.g. CorelDraw. (Microsoft is either a registered trademark of Microsoft Corporation in the United States and/or other countries.)

(c) Any reasonable answer, for example: clip art can be imported; word art can be generated; shapes can be automatically filled with different colours or patterns; borders can be automatically generated.

(d) Any reasonable answer, for example: the name of the clothes shop; where the sale is; when the sale is; the items reduced.

Question 7

(a) Any reasonable answer, for example: *Advantage*: the student can talk to native speakers of Japanese. *Disadvantage*: the technology is currently too slow so that speech is slightly distorted.

(b) Any reasonable answer, for example: *Advantage*: a doctor can treat the oil rig worker immediately using video conferencing. *Disadvantage*: treatment via video conferencing is unlikely to be as effective as treatment by a doctor on site.

(c) Any reasonable answer, for example: *Advantage*: young people can be taught at home. *Disadvantage*: young people do not meet their school friends other than by a video conferencing link.

Question 8

(a) Any reasonable answer, for example: the journalist can prepare an article at the scene of a newsworthy incident using a portable computer and a wordprocessor; the journalist can use e-mail to transmit the article over long distances more quickly.

(b) Any reasonable answer, for example: using graphic software the designer can manipulate images faster than using pencil and paper; graphic tools that generate standard shapes, such as rectangles, allow new designs to be created more easily.

(c) Any reasonable answer, for example: town plans can be more easily edited to explore the effects of new roads; plans can be stored indefinitely without deteriorating.

Question 9 – Student answer

(a) Columns; pixels.

> **Examiner's note** The first answer is correct. The second answer should be 'Clip art'.

(b) A laser printer costs less to buy than a dot matrix printer.

> **Examiner's note** This answer could be true in the exceptional case where the prices of a very cheap laser printer and a very expensive dot matrix printer are compared, but it is not generally true. 'A laser printer prints good quality text and graphics' is a better answer as this is always true in comparison with the poorer quality of a dot matrix printer.

(c) The Tennis club should not use IT as it does not have a computer already and will have to buy one.

> **Examiner's note** In the context of the question, this answer is not correct as we know from part (a) that the secretary has access to DTP software. It is starting to make the point that the cost of a computer system has to be measured against various positive improvements, such as better quality presentation and more efficient administration. However, this is not a well 'reasoned argument'. As there are 4 marks available, I would advise making four well-reasoned points.

Question 10 – Student answer

(a) Feature 1: can import clip art.
Part of the poster it was used to produce: the face is probably an imported clip art image.

> **Examiner's note** A good answer showing a mastery of technical language.

Feature 2: bubbles.
Part of the poster it was used to produce: the thinking bubbles.

> **Examiner's note** The student would have probably had more success choosing a feature where the precise technical language was known. 'Bubbles' is not the appropriate term for the DTP tools that enable users to create standard shapes, such as the ellipses that are shown.

(b) Software 1: wordprocessor.
Software 2: spreadsheet.

> **Examiner's note** The student has not read the question thoroughly and has not noticed that wordprocessing software has been specifically excluded. It is easy to make this mistake as only DTP software is referred to in part (a). Even so, no marks would be given for the first answer. The second answer is correct.

(c) A spreadsheet will be used to keep track of all the money earned and all the money spent. Details of every purchase and sale will need to be kept.

> **Examiner's note** A good answer.

2 Solutions
Handling information and databases

SOLUTIONS TO REVISION ACTIVITIES

Question 1
– Information about a car's owner can be accessed from a moving police car by typing in the car's registration number.
– At an estate agents, a list of houses that meet a client's needs can be quickly found and printed.
– An overall summary of a school's GCSE results can be made very quickly from records of each pupil's results.

Question 2
3. Data is coded to save storage space.

Question 3
(a) – Name begins with 'K': 119.
– Member_Number contains '9': 098, 119, 099.
– Subscription_Outstanding is more than 20.00: 237, 119.
– Name begins with 'R' AND Member_Category is Full: 876.
– Member_Category is NOT Honorary: 237, 098, 035, 119, 876.
– Name begins with 'J' OR Member_Category is Honorary: 237, 098, 099.
(b) Jones, Paul; Kosar, Roksana; Rodin, Selvar; Majid, Rizwan; Jackson, Jean; Robinson, Martin.

(c) F=Full; S=Student; H=Honorary.
(d) – The form has a heading and a preamble explaining its purpose.
    – It requests and has space to enter the member's name and the membership category required.
    – The subscription required is shown and related to the membership category.
    – Boxes are used for filling in appropriate parts of the questionnaire, e.g. the member's name.
    – Tick lists are used for filling in appropriate parts of the questionnaire, e.g. the membership category.
    – There is space to sign and date the questionnaire.
    – There is a space for writing the membership number on the questionnaire after it has been generated by the database.
(e) Any reasonable answer, for example:
Is Member_Number between 001 and 999 inclusive?

Question 4
(a) Any reasonable answer, for example: news, weather forecast, share prices.
(b) Ceefax or Oracle.
(c) Any reasonable answer, for example: using a remote control, press the teletext button and type in the page number of the information required.
(d) Any reasonable answer, for example: *Advantage*: teletext is a free information service. *Disadvantage*: teletext is slow as pages are transmitted one after the other in order.

Question 5
(a) Any reasonable answer, for example: the Internet is an international network of interconnected networks, including the telephone network. It can be accessed from home using a desktop PC, a browser such as Netscape, a modem and a subscription to an Internet Service Provider, e.g. Compuserve. You would connect to the Internet via a connection to the Internet Service Provider.
(b) Any reasonable answer, for example: information about courses at Huddersfield University; the Yellow Pages; the national railway timetable.
(c) Information can be accessed by: connection to a specific WWW information server using its Uniform Resource Locator (URL); 'surfing' the WWW, that is, by wandering from information server to information server; searching for particular topics using a search engine, for example, Yahoo.

SOLUTIONS TO PRACTICE QUESTIONS

Question 1
(a) A field; a name; a scanned image.
(b) – You can quickly search the information to find out what you want to know.
    – The space needed to store a large volume of information on a database is much less than if it was written down.
    – Large volumes of information stored on a database can be copied and sent around the world much faster and at less cost than on paper.

Question 2
(a) (i)   12th February 1985 = 850212.
    (ii) 6th December 2000 = 001206.
(b) (i)   970113 = 13th January 1997.
    (ii) 451013 = 13th October 1945.
(c) (i)   871301 is invalid as there is not a month 13.
    (ii) 791232 is invalid as there is not a 32nd of December.
    (iii) 260231 is invalid as there is never a 31st of February.

Question 3

(a) – You access information on teletext by entering a page number.
- You may have to wait for the page you want as they are broadcast in cycle.

(b) – Fastext permits faster access to some teletext pages using a TV with additional RAM memory installed. When a page is selected it is displayed on the TV screen as normal but, in addition, adjacent pages are stored in memory. These pages will be displayed instantaneously if selected whereas other pages will not be displayed any faster than on a TV without fastext.

(c) Any reasonable answer, for example: teletext pages can be downloaded and stored on backing storage for later reference; share prices downloaded from teletext can be processed to produce graphs, etc.

Question 4

(a) Any reasonable answer, for example:
- A Book file which contains information about the books. Typical fields are: book number, author, title, location, etc.
- A Members file which contains information about members. Typical fields are: member number, member's name, address, membership category, etc.
- A Loans file which links the books on loan to the members who have borrowed them. Typical fields are: book number, member number.

(b) (i) – The new members' form has a heading and a preamble explaining its purpose.
- It requests and has space to enter, at least, the member's name and the membership category required. Other useful fields are shown, e.g. member's address.
- Boxes are used for filling in appropriate parts of the form, e.g. the member's name.
- Tick lists are used for filling in appropriate parts of the form, e.g. the membership category.
- There is space to sign and date the form.
- There is a space for writing the member's number on the form after it has been generated by the library's IT system.

(ii) – The book request form has a heading and a preamble explaining its purpose.
- It requests and has space to enter, at least, the member's number and the book number required. Other useful fields are shown, e.g. member's name and address.
- Boxes are used for filling in appropriate parts of the form, e.g. the member's number.
- There is space to sign and date the form.
- The form is also a postcard that can be sent to members to notify them that the book they have requested has arrived.

(c) Any reasonable answer, for example: a library membership card might also be a swipe card with a bar code or a magnetic stripe. It would have on it the name of the library, and the member's name and number. It might also have a photograph of the member, the location of the library, how to contact the library, and what to do with the card if it is found when lost.

(d) Any reasonable answer, for example: verification could be built into the normal operation of the system. If the member's card has on it the member's name and address as entered from the new members' form, the member could verify that the details entered into the computer are accurate when the card is received.

(e) Any reasonable answer, for example: if a bar code is used on the member's card to encode the member's number, when this is read a check digit could be used to ensure that a valid number has been input.

(f) Any reasonable answer, for example: the librarian would want a list of overdue books and the member numbers, names and addresses of the members who have not returned them on time. The librarian needs this information so that these members can be reminded to return their books and of possible fines if they do not.

(g) (i) Any reasonable answer, for example: the overdue notices may not be received by members whose addresses are incorrect.

(ii) Any reasonable answer, for example: the library could print out the information it has stored about each member and ask them to check that it is accurate. If necessary, this could be done annually by post.

Question 5

(a) Pupil; seven; alphanumeric.

(b) (i) Pupil_Number.

(ii) A key field is used to identify a pupil's record.

(iii) The key field must be unique. The database knows which key fields have already been used and can check that the new key field is not already in use.

(c) (i) G=good; E=epilepsy; A=asthma.

(ii) Any reasonable answer, for example: a code could occupy less space on backing storage making the file more compact; a code could be quicker to type in at a keyboard.

(iii) Any reasonable answer, for example: uses a tick list showing each state of health which has an 'other' alternative at the end of the list with space to explain what the other state of health is.

(d) (i) Any reasonable answer, for example: Sex is M or Sex is F.

(ii) Any reasonable answer, for example: Is Pupil_Number an integer?; Is Pupil_Number between 0001 and 9999 inclusive?

(e) (i) Ascending order on the Name field:
Dean, N; Dobson, J; Ellis, M; Grant, K; Jackson, P; Patel, M; Singh, R; Wall, R.

(iii) Descending order on the Pupil_Number field:
0056 Patel, M; 1045 Dobson, J; 1057 Ellis, M; 1874 Dean, N; 2001 Singh, R; 2045 Jackson, P; 2343 Grant, K; 4892 Wall, R.

(f) (i) Health is NOT 'good': Dean, N; Patel, M; Grant, K.

(ii) Sex is NOT 'M': Grant, K; Wall, R.

(iii) Sex is 'M' AND Form is '*WE'; Singh, R.

(iv) Name begins with 'D' AND Form is '7EG': Dobson, J.

(v) Form is '7EG' OR Area is 'Thornton': Jackson, P; Wall, R.

(vi) Health is 'Epilepsy' OR Sex is 'F': Dean, N; Grant, K; Wall, R.

(vii) Form is '7EG' AND Days Absent is NOT bigger than 2: Jackson, P; Dobson, J.

(viii) (Form is '9GH' AND Sex is 'M') OR Area is 'Queensbury': Dean, N; Patel, M; Grant, K.

(g) Any reasonable answer, for example:

(i) – Sex is M.
– The teacher in charge of boys sports may need this information.
– It might best be printed in ascending alphabetic order.
– The Name and Form fields would be needed.

(ii) – Sex is M AND Days_Absent is more than 3.
– The teacher in charge of boys attendance may need this information.
– It might best be printed in ascending alphabetic order.
– The Name, Form and Days_Absent fields would be needed.

(iii) – Area is Allerton.
– The transport employee organising school buses may need this information.
– It might best be printed in ascending alphabetic order.
– The Name, Form and Sex fields would be needed.

(iv) – Area is Allerton AND Days_Absent is more than 3.
  – The educational welfare officer responsible for school attendance for the Allerton area may need this information.
  – It might best be printed in ascending alphabetic order.
  – The Name, Form and Sex fields would be needed. Pupils' addresses would also be needed.

(v) – Form is 9GH and Sex is F.
  – A teacher trying to find out which girls were in the library in period 2 when 9GH were timetabled to be there may need this information.
  – It might best be printed in ascending alphabetic order.
  – The Name field would be needed.

(vi) – Form is 7EG and Sex is M.
  – A teacher trying to find out which boys were in the gym in period 3 when 9GH were timetabled to be there may need this information.
  – It might best be printed in ascending alphabetic order.
  – The Name field would be needed.

(vii) – Health is good (or Health is G if you assume Health has been coded).
  – A teacher trying to find out which pupils will be fit enough to participate in the annual school half marathon run may need this information.
  – It might best be printed with pupils' Names in ascending alphabetic order within their Forms printed in ascending form order.
  – The Name, Form and Sex fields would be needed.

(viii) – Health is A AND Area is Denholme.
  – The school nurse who wants to inform pupils of a special clinic for asthma sufferers to be held in Denholme.
  – It might best be printed with pupils' Names in ascending alphabetic order within their Forms printed in ascending form order.
  – The Name, Form and Sex fields would be needed. Pupils' addresses would also be needed.

(ix) – Area is Queensbury OR Area is Denholme.
  – The transport employee organizing school buses may need this information.
  – It might best be printed in ascending alphabetic order.
  – The Name, Form and Sex fields would be needed.

(h) (i) Any reasonable answer, for example: A teacher looking for a pupil could go to the wrong form.

(ii) Any reasonable answer, for example: The school could print out the information for each pupil separately. This could be given to pupils or sent to their parents with a request to check it and inform the school if it is incorrect.

Question 6

(a) (i) Double entry verification involves these steps:
  – The information is entered a first time, usually via the keyboard.
  – The same information is entered a second time.
  – The computer checks that the information entered the first time is the same as the information entered the second time. If it is not, an input error has occurred and this must be corrected before further processing can take place.

(ii) To check that what is entered into the computer is entered accurately.

(iii) Any reasonable answer, for example: there is only a very small probability that the information entered has not been entered accurately.

(iv) Any reasonable answer, for example: it can be expensive and time consuming as the task of entering the information has to be done twice.

(b) (i) Any reasonable answer, for example: a range check, $0<MM<13$.

(ii) Any reasonable answer, for example: a check digit.

(iii) Any reasonable answer, for example: check that the signature on the transaction slip matches that on the credit card.

Question 7

(a) Ceefax, Oracle.

(b) Any reasonable answer, for example: news, weather forecast, TV programmes, lottery numbers, football results, share prices.

(c) Any reasonable answer, for example: a walker who was going to the Yorkshire Dales might want to know what the weather forecast is before setting off; a young child might want to know what children's programmes were being shown on a Saturday morning so they would know what time to get up.

(d) Any reasonable answer, for example: type in the number on the remote control.

(e) The pages are broadcast in a cycle. If, for example, page 301 has just been broadcast and you have just entered page 300, you will have to wait until all the pages in the cycle have been broadcast before page 300 is displayed.

(f) Fastext permits faster access to some teletext pages using a TV with additional RAM memory installed. When a page is selected it is displayed on the TV screen as normal but, in addition, adjacent pages are stored in memory. These pages will be displayed instantaneously if selected whereas other pages that are not in memory will not be displayed any faster than on a TV without fastext.

(g) Teletext is not interactive. You can enter page numbers to select pages but this only helps you navigate the information. You cannot otherwise interact with teletext.

(h) Any reasonable answer, for example: *Advantage*: teletext pages can be downloaded and stored on backing storage for later reference. *Disadvantage*: If you already have a TV with teletext, you must spend more on a teletext card for your computer.

Question 8

(a) The Internet is a worldwide collection of interconnected computer networks.

(b) Any reasonable answer, for example: from home you would need a modem and cables, a telephone point, browser software or similar, and a subscription to an Internet service provider.

(c) The WWW is the multimedia information service that runs on the Internet. The information is provided by an ad hoc collection of information servers which can be accessed using browser software, e.g. Netscape.

(d) (i) Any reasonable answer, for example: school inspection reports, bed and breakfast establishments, on-line shopping.

    (ii) Any reasonable answer, for example: The Daily Telegraph, http://www.telegraph.co.uk; The Yahoo Internet search engine, http://www.yahoo.com; The French ministry of culture, http://www.culture.fr.

    (iii) Any reasonable answer, for example: *Advantage*: it is faster as you can access a specific site directly without searching or surfing. *Disadvantage*: you may make errors typing in the URL as it can be long and complex.

(e) (i) Any reasonable answer, for example:
1. Connect to the Yahoo search engine's WWW site by typing in its URL.
2. Type in the search condition, click on the search button, and wait for a response.
3. Look through the list of relevant references returned to see if one is suitable.
4. If one is suitable, access it using its hot spot; if none are relevant or too many references are returned, then refine your search condition and return to step 2.

    (ii) Any reasonable answer, for example: *Advantage*: the search engine may find useful material you were not aware of. *Disadvantage*: the search engine may take a long time searching the WWW.

(f) (i) Any reasonable answer, for example: wandering the WWW by accessing one information server after another by moving from hotspot to hotspot.

(ii) Any reasonable answer, for example: *Advantage*: when you surf, you follow your interests and the browser tracks you. Your route can be kept for other occasions so you can refer back to the wealth of interesting information you find. *Disadvantage*: surfing is unlikely to be systematic or thorough, so you may miss some useful information sources.

(iii) Any reasonable answer, for example: parents may be concerned that their children will access unsuitable material, e.g. pornography.

Question 9 – Student answer

(a) (i) {Find Cargo starts with meth}.

Examiner's note Incorrect. This search condition would find methanol but not machine tools, meal and meat. Unfortunately, it is not the shortest search condition. This is {Find Cargo starts with met}.

(ii) Because it selects only those records where the contents of the Cargo field start with meth.

Examiner's notes Correct. This answer shows a good understanding of the question and uses appropriate technical language. The use of 'meth' instead of 'met' would be ignored here, even though it is not quite accurate, as marks for getting this incorrect were lost in part (i).

(iii) Because other goods could start with meth.

Examiner's note Correct. Again the use of 'meth' instead of 'met' would be ignored. However, if the student wants to demonstrate a clear understanding of the question, it would be better to give an example of these other goods, such as 'methane gas'.

(b) (i) Meat and meal are not carried at the same time.

Examiner's note The student's answer is a true statement but does not answer the question. The question actually refers to the operation of the search condition. As the Cargo field can only contain either 'meat' or 'meal' but not both, the AND operation will never find a field that contains both of them.

(ii) {Find Cargo is 'meat' OR Cargo is 'meal'}.

Examiner's note Correct. This search condition will select those records where the Cargo field contains either 'meat' or 'meal'.

(c) VANTEC would ask people to fill in the questionnaire. This might use OMR so that the answers could be input into the computer without spending time typing them in. The results could be worked out using a database or a spreadsheet.

Examiner's note This is a reasonable answer but slightly off the point. The student has concentrated on how the data is collected and input rather than on how the data is analysed. The frequency of particular responses and combinations of responses could be analysed using a database, and the ability of a spreadsheet to produce tables and graphs should be mentioned.

Question 10 – Student answer

(a) (i) A minimum age of 116 is circled.

Examiner's note Correct.

(ii) *People do not live that long.*

Examiner's note Correct.

(b) *Advantage 1. You can find a job faster.*
Advantage 2. No jobs will get taken by other people.
Advantage 3. It is more efficient.

Examiner's note Advantage 1. Too vague. Even with a database it might take a long time to find a job. The student probably means that it is possible to search a database more quickly using a search condition (or query) that states the type of job the student is interested in.

Advantage 2. Too vague. The student probably means that other people cannot take the details for jobs they want off a database whereas they can remove cards pinned to the walls.

Advantage 3. Answers like these are given no marks unless they go on to explain why or in what way 'it is more efficient'.

(c) *Pay > 10000.*

Examiner's note Correct. Notice that the answer uses the fieldname given in the table and the number format used in the table.

(d) *Age >= 18 AND Type of job = "Sales" OR Pay > 13000.*

Examiner's note There are two mistakes is this query. The fieldname 'Minimum age' should have been used and the OR operation should be AND.

3

Solutions
Modelling and spreadsheets

SOLUTIONS TO REVISION ACTIVITIES

Question 1
Rows; columns; cell.

Question 2
Text, formulae, dates, numbers.

Question 3
– Relative cell references will adjust automatically when formulae are copied from one cell to another.
– Formulae may recalculate automatically when the numbers in the cells they refer to change.
– An absolute cell reference will not change when it is moved or copied to a new position.

Question 4
(a) (i) Any reasonable answer, for example: A1.
   (ii) Any reasonable answer, for example: D3.
(b) Any reasonable answer, for example: (B3+C3+D3)/3.

(c)

Dobson	50	56	45	50.3
Edwards	55	54	53	54.0
Harris	44	34	42	40.0
Patel	57	23	45	41.7
Singh	70	67	68	68.3
Sweryt	65	52	62	59.7

(d) Run the spreadsheet; highlight the graph; copy the graph; run the wordprocessor; paste the graph.

(e) Any reasonable answer, for example: this could save time as a spreadsheet template could be set up to analyse any set of examination results.

Question 5

(a) Any reasonable answer, for example: using a model steering wheel, and pedals that simulate the accelerator and brakes.

(b) – If a car runs out of petrol, the game is over.
   – If a car leaves the track, it crashes.
   – If a car crashes four times, the game is over.

(c) Any reasonable answer, for example: the learner driver could learn how to use a steering wheel.

SOLUTIONS TO PRACTICE QUESTIONS

Question 1

(a) Formula, number, text.

(b) Bar charts, calculations, pie charts.

(c) – Constructing a predator/prey model.
   – Working out the cost of making a cake.
   – Reporting on the profits made by a business.

(d) – Line graphs can be generated more easily than drawing them by hand.
   – Formulae are calculated and re-calculated automatically.
   – Relative cell references are adjusted automatically when formulae are copied from one cell to another.

(e) – If you want to use a spreadsheet you must have access to a computer.
   – You have to know how to use a spreadsheet.
   – If you want to use a spreadsheet you must be able to use a computer.

Question 2

(a) (i) Any reasonable answer, for example: B1.
   (ii) Any reasonable answer, for example: B5.

(b) Any reasonable answer, for example: SUM(C2:C6).

(c) Tue (Tuesday).

(d) Any reasonable answer, for example: the columns will be added up without errors.

(e) Any reasonable answer, for example: it may be more convenient to count the money taken and write this down as there is no access to a computer in the tuck shop.

Question 3

(a) (i)   Any reasonable answer, for example: C5*D5.
   (ii) Any reasonable answer, for example: SUM(E4:E7).
   (iii) Any reasonable answer, for example: (C6-B6)*D6.
   (iv) Any reasonable answer, for example: SUM(F4:F7).
   (v)   Any reasonable answer, for example: 100*F4/E4.

(b) Any reasonable answer, for example: the value of profits would be incorrect, and as a result the shopkeeper may spend more money than is available to spend.

(c) (i)

Bran Flakes	0.85	0.95	53	50.35	5.30	10.5
Corn Flakes	0.78	1.05	124	130.20	33.48	25.7
Muesli	1.70	1.95	85	165.75	21.25	12.8
Porridge	0.80	0.90	65	58.50	6.50	11.1

(ii) Any reasonable answer, for example: the spreadsheet should be saved.

Figure A3.2   (d) (i)

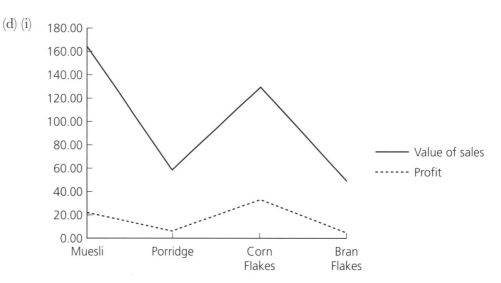

(ii) Any reasonable answer, for example: the graph would help the shopkeeper compare the profits made with the value of sales. This might help the shopkeeper identify those goods which have the best profit margins.

(iii) Any reasonable answer, for example: save the report; open the spreadsheet; copy the graph; close the spreadsheet; paste the graph into the wordprocessor.

(e) Any reasonable answer, for example: *Advantage*: the shopkeeper can be confident the calculations have been done accurately. *Disadvantage*: the shopkeeper must have access to a computer, and be able to use it.

Question 4

(a) (i) Any reasonable answer, for example: A1, A6.

(ii) Any reasonable answer, for example: B4, C4.

(b) Rate of interest, in cell B1.

(c) Any reasonable answer, for example: because the value in it is an input variable.

(d) Any reasonable answer, for example: SUM(D4:D5).

(e) Any reasonable answer, for example: B6.

(f) Any reasonable answer, for example: B4*B1/100. B4 is a relative cell reference; B1 is the absolute cell reference for cell B1.

(g) Any reasonable answer, for example: no this is not a reasonable assumption as the rate of interest paid on savings accounts tends to change once or twice a year.

(h) Any reasonable answer, for example: assuming both the spreadsheet and the wordprocessor are running, *in the spreadsheet window*: highlight cells A1:D6; in the edit menu, select copy; *in the wordprocessor window*: put the cursor where the cells are to be placed; *from the edit menu*, select paste.

Question 5

A flight simulator could be used to learn to fly an aeroplane.

A pilot could use a flight simulator to see how an aeroplane would perform in different weather conditions.

A flight simulator could be used to see what it is like to fly different aeroplanes.

Question 6

(a) – As the amount of insecticide sprayed goes up, the number of insects killed goes up.
  – As the number of insects attacking the crop goes down, the crop yield goes up.

(b) Any reasonable answer, for example: the farmer could work out how much insecticide should be sprayed to get the largest increase in yield with an acceptable crop quality.

(c) Any reasonable answer, for example: the rules programmed into the model might not take into account all the environmental influences. If the farmer acted on the model's predictions, the amount of insecticide sprayed might not control the insects satisfactorily.

Question 7

(a) Any reasonable answer, for example: *Manual method*: a person counts the number of checkouts in use and enters it into the computer. *Automatic method*: the checkouts are networked so the computer can tell if they are in use.

(b) – All the checkout operators work at the same speed all the time.
  – All the checkouts in use can be operated at the same speed.
  – Equal numbers of customers queue at each checkout.

(c) (i) 28 minutes.
   (ii) 16 minutes.

(d) Any reasonable answer, for example: *Manual method*: the time to serve each customer in a sample is measured by a person using a stopwatch. The average time is assumed to be the total time divided by the number of customers in the sample. *Automatic method*: the computer counts the number of customers and records the time for every customer from the first item scanned to the end of the receipt being printed. The average time is the total time divided by the number of customers.

(e) Any reasonable answer, for example:

	A	B
1	DIY superstore	
2		
3	Total number of customers waiting	21
4	Number of checkouts in use	3
5	Average number of customers at each checkout	=B3/B4
6	Average time to serve each customer	4
7	Queuing time for the last customer in the queue	=B5*B6

Question 8 – Student answer

(a) (i) A.

> **Examiner's note** Incorrect. Ambulance A will take 11 minutes to get to the emergency; B will take 8 minutes; C will take 16 minutes. The ambulance that will get to the emergency the quickest should be chosen, that is B.

   (ii) The time it will take for each ambulance to get to the emergency. An indication whether the medical supplies carried will allow an ambulance to deal with the emergency.

> **Examiner's note** Correct.

(iii) *Assumption 1: The ambulance has enough petrol.*
Assumption 2: The driver does not stop for lunch.

Examiner's note Assumption 1 is clearly correct but assumption 2 is doubtful. The model would probably not include ambulances if the driver is taking a break. The student may be expressing the assumption that the model will expect that ambulances travel at average speeds for the road.

(b) (i) *2.00 × 50.*

Examiner's note Incorrect, this is not a formula but the calculation that would be done by the spreadsheet. A correct formula is B3*C3.

(ii) *1415.00 + 100.00 + 220.00.*

Examiner's note Incorrect for the same reason as in part (i). A correct answer is SUM(D2:D4).

(iii) *707.50; text; a number.*

Examiner's note 707.50 is not in the list so it cannot be correct. The correct answer is a 'number'. 'Text' is correct. Numbers are never recalculated as they always have a particular value in a spreadsheet cell. The correct answer is 'a formula'.

(iv) *You would look at the total value to see if it is below £1400. If it isn't you would have to reduce the quantity of medical supplies carried and see if this brought the total value down far enough.*

Examiner's note This is a good answer but it is not complete. The hospital could also buy in the medical supplies at lower unit costs. The spreadsheet could show the hospital which unit costs have the most impact on overall costs.

(c) *Problems; costs; reports.*

Examiner's note Correct.

Question 9 – Student answer

(a) *25.*

Examiner's note Correct.

(b) (i) *Sum(G4:G15).*

Examiner's note The student has misunderstood the question and added the Total Costs column. The correct answer adds columns D, E and F in any row, e.g. D4 + E4 + F4.

(ii) *Profits = Income – Total Costs.*

Examiner's note This is a good general answer but in relation to this spreadsheet does not go far enough. An example of a correct answer is C15 – G15.

(c) *C.*

Examiner's note Correct but incomplete. H is also correct.

(d) *A spreadsheet can be used for booking airline tickets.*

Examiner's note A spreadsheet could be used for booking airline tickets, and this might happen in a hotel, but this is not a good answer. A better answer would refer to activities that are central to the operation of a hotel, for example, booking rooms.

4 Solutions
Monitoring and control

★ SOLUTIONS TO REVISION ACTIVITIES

Question 1
Input, measure; output, adjust; recording, storage.

Question 2
Wind speed, air humidity, soil temperature.

Question 3
Motor, boiler, switch, heater, valve, pump.

Question 4
(a) START
    OPEN
    DOWN 6
    CLOSE
    UP 3
    END
(b) Any reasonable answer, for example: the closed claws descend onto the object and attempt to crush it.

Question 5
10 seconds; half hour; day.

SOLUTIONS TO PRACTICE QUESTIONS

Question 1
(a) Microswitches on windows; pressure pads under carpets; Passive Infra Red detectors (PIRs) mounted on walls.
(b) Any reasonable answer, for example; an alarm, a flashing light.
(c) Any reasonable answer, for example: adjust the sensitivity of the system so that it detects a burglar but not a cat, for example, the weight of a cat on a pressure pad should not set off the alarm but the weight of a burglar should.

Question 2
(a) You should have drawn a rectangle measuring 5 paces by 2 paces.
(b) Any reasonable answer, for example:
    FORWARD 2 PACES.
    TURN LEFT 90 DEGREES.
    REPEAT 2 TIMES [FORWARD 2 PACES TURN RIGHT 90 DEGREES].
    FORWARD 2 PACES.
    TURN LEFT 90 DEGREES.
    REPEAT 2 TIMES [FORWARD 2 PACES TURN RIGHT 90 DEGREES].
    FORWARD 6 PACES.
    TURN RIGHT 90 DEGREES.
    FORWARD 2 PACES.

(c) You should have drawn an equilateral triangle with sides 4 paces long.

(d) Any reasonable answer, for example:
   REPEAT 4 TIMES [FORWARD 2 PACES TURN RIGHT 90 DEGREES].

Question 3

(a) Any reasonable answer, for example: it has heat sensors connected to it.

(b) Any reasonable answer, for example: switch on the heater.

(c) IF TEMPERATURE IS MORE THAN SET_LEVEL THEN TURN HEATER OFF.

(d) Line 3 would be changed to SET_LEVEL = 21.

(e) Any reasonable answer, for example: *Advantage*: they can control the temperature in their buildings and the costs involved. *Disadvantage*: if employees open the windows, the heating may be automatically turned on and energy wasted.

(f) Any reasonable answer, for example: *Advantage*: the temperature is maintained at a comfortable level. *Disadvantage*: the temperature is not under their control.

(g) Any reasonable answer, for example: *Advantage*: they only pay for the engineer when they need work doing. *Disadvantage*: the engineer may not be available immediately when needed.

(h) Reliable, easy to maintain.

Question 4

(a) – To show how temperature changes when water is heated, 10 seconds, 10 minutes.
   – To show how sound levels due to traffic change on a busy main street; 20 minutes; 1 week.
   – To show how the number of hours of daylight each day changes throughout the year; 1 hour; 1 year.

(b) (i) Wind speed, temperature, humidity.
   (ii) Any reasonable answer, for example: as information is recorded at the weather station it is saved on backing storage; every week, the main computer connects to the weather station and downloads the information.
   (iii) Any reasonable answer, for example: weather forecasting; regulating the artificial nutrients automatically added to crop sprays.
   (iv) Any reasonable answer, for example: *Advantage*: more information can be collected across a wider area more quickly. *Disadvantage*: IT can only sense and record what it is set up to do. As a result, some relevant information may not be recorded.

Question 5

(a) A heat sensor.

(b) A heater.

(c) Any reasonable diagram showing, for example: see Figure 4.1 on p. 41.

(d) Any reasonable answer, for example: feedback is a cycle of sensing, processing and reaction. The computer uses the heat sensor to sense the temperature in the incubator. If the temperature is too high it turns off the heater; if the temperature is too low it turns on the heater.

(e) Any reasonable answer, for example: the chicks could be injured or die.

(f) Any reasonable answer, for example: *Advantage*: a constant temperature will be maintained. *Disadvantage*: if the temperature is set too high or too low, this will also be maintained.

Question 6

(a) (i) The total number of cars is increased by one.
   (ii) The total number of cars is reduced by one.

(b) Total number of cars in the car park = total –1 for each car leaving +1 for each car entering.

(c) Any reasonable answer, for example: IF the number of cars in the car park IS NOT LESS THAN 50 do not raise the barrier.

(d) (i) Any reasonable answer, for example: some cars stayed in the car park overnight.

   (ii) Any reasonable answer, for example: count the number of cars in the car park and enter this into the computer.

(e) Any reasonable answer, for example: when the entrance barrier is raised, two cars enter the car park but the computer only counts this as one car.

Question 7

(a) Any reasonable answer, for example:

Figure A4.1

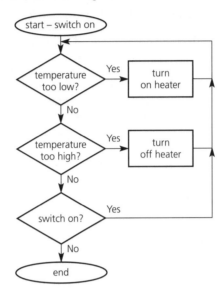

(b) Any reasonable answer, for example:
START
REPEAT UNTIL THE FRIDGE IS SWITCHED OFF
    [IF THE TEMPERATURE IS TOO LOW THEN TURN ON THE HEATER
    IF THE TEMPERATURE IS TOO HIGH THEN TURN OFF THE HEATER]
END

(c) Any reasonable answer, for example: feedback is a cycle of sensing, processing and reaction. The computer uses a heat sensor to sense the temperature in the fridge. If the temperature is too high it turns off the heater; if the temperature is too low it turns on the heater.

Question 8

(a) Conditional statement; loop; procedure.

(b) (i) Any reasonable answer, for example: you would use a loop for any sequence of instructions that are repeated, for example, monitoring the temperature in a fridge (see the answer to Question 7 above).

   (ii) Any reasonable answer, for example: a procedure is used where a particular task needs doing several times at different stages in a computer program or in several programs. For example, calculating VAT.

   (iii) Any reasonable answer, for example: a conditional statement is used if what the instruction does depends on some condition, for example:
   IF THE TEMPERATURE IS TOO HIGH THEN TURN OFF THE HEATER

Question 9 – Student answer

(a) S2 W7.

> **Examiner's note** Incorrect. This answer may appear to move the crane from A to B but, unfortunately, it does not take into account that the crane will probably not float in the sea.

(b) The computer should know that the crane will go in the sea and should tell the human operator that it won't do it.

> **Examiner's note** A good answer. The computer should know the limits of operation of the crane and should alert operators to programmed activity outside these limits. Other acceptable answers might be based on the difference between the format of the instruction 4 N and the example instructions. The computer may not like instructions in this new format and may alert the human operator and ask him/her to use the example format.

(c) The computer will need to be connected to sensors that can detect the object and tell it how big it is.

> **Examiner's note** A reasonable answer. Perhaps the student could have mentioned the type of sensors required, for example, video cameras with pattern recognition software. 'Big' is almost too vague as we are probably more concerned about the width and frontal shape of the object.

(d) (i) Feedback occurs when a sensor senses information about a situation that requires the computer to take action to alter the situation. The action taken changes the situation and, in consequence, the information sensed by the sensor.

> **Examiner's note** This is a text book answer. Note that the question asked what is meant 'in this context'. The student has not mentioned the context and could not expect to get full marks.

(ii) Without feedback the crane would not know where it was.

> **Examiner's note** A poor answer which would reinforce the impression given in part (i) that this student does not really understand the concept of feedback. The computer could know where the crane was without using feedback, however, it could not automatically guide the crane round objects unless it received feedback on their position and size as it moved.

(e) Advantage in having a human operator: a human operator could see the position of the crane and the object and would know what instructions to give. Advantage in having an automatic system: the computer is more reliable than a human operator as it is constantly alert.

> **Examiner's note** Advantage in having a human operator: true, but an automatic control system could also do this task. The real advantage of a human operator is that he/she will be aware of features of the object that an automatic system might not pick up. For example, the difference between a crate and a crowd of people. Advantage in having an automatic system: A good answer.

Question 10 – Student answer

(a) Mr Smith could be sick or late and not collect the data.

> **Examiner's note** A good answer but this is really only one problem, that is, Mr Smith does not collect the data every day at the same time. Other problems are that Mr Smith is limited to data that is collected during the day, and could only collect data once or twice a day at most.

(b) Data logging software.

> *Examiner's note* Correct.

(c) (i) Printer; sensors.

> *Examiner's note* A printer will not help Mr Smith collect the data but a range of sensors for light, wind speed, etc. and a control interface would be very useful.

(ii) Hard disk; floppy disk.

> *Examiner's note* Correct, but a better answer would have mentioned two distinctly different items of hardware.

(d) There would be sensors for temperature and soil moisture in the greenhouse. These would connect to a control interface which is connected to the computer. If the greenhouse is too hot, the computer will tell the actuators to turn off the heat and open the windows. If the greenhouse is too moist, the computer will turn off the water spray and open the windows.

> *Examiner's note* A reasonable answer. However, the student has not mentioned what will happen if the greenhouse is too cold or too dry. In addition, the student has not mentioned the need for a control program or given pseudo code instructions to show what this would look like.

5 Solutions
Applications

★ SOLUTIONS TO REVISION ACTIVITIES

Question 1
(a) MICR.
(b) The amount.

Question 2
(a) A missile guidance system; a computer-controlled robot welder; a flight simulator for training pilots.
(b) Quickly; dedicated; before.

Question 3
(a) Systems investigation; implementation; evaluation.
(b) – The information provided was inaccurate.
   – Mistakes were made when the information was entered into the computer.
   – The information has become out-of-date.

Question 4
(a) The book's identity number; a check digit.
(b) – The library can print a list of overdue books automatically.
   – It is faster to find a book using an on-line library catalogue.
   – Borrowers can get more information about books using an on-line library catalogue.

Question 5

(a) Technical documentation; this would be used by technicians and other specialists who keep the IT system running.

University documentation; this would be used by the people who use the IT system to handle hotel bookings.

(b) Any reasonable answer, for example: a bug in the IT system may not have been found during testing; the IT system needs extending so that it can do some task it cannot do at present.

SOLUTIONS TO PRACTICE QUESTIONS

Question 1

(a) Country of origin; check digit; product code.

(b) Total to pay; price of goods; quantity purchased.

(c) Any reasonable answer, for example: the product code is input at the checkout; the product code is sent to the main computer; the product code is used to find the product's record in the product file; the product's description is sent to the checkout; the product's description is printed on the receipt.

(d) – Customers are more likely to be charged the correct price.
   – Customers get more information about their purchases.
   – The supermarket can change prices faster and more consistently.

(e) Any reasonable answer, for example: the number of each product in stock is input to the computer; as stock is sold at the checkout, this is automatically deducted; as stock arrives at the warehouse, this is entered in the computer.

(f) Any reasonable answer, for example: the computer knows the re-order level for each product; when the number in stock falls below the re-order level, the product is re-ordered; the supermarket's computer can automatically dial up the supplier's computer and place an order.

(g) On-line; interactive, multiaccess.

Question 2

(a) Phone card; cheque guarantee card; cashless payment.

(b) Magnetic stripe.

(c) Any reasonable answer, for example: put the plastic card in the slot; enter your PIN number; select the option that lets you withdraw money; enter the amount of money; wait for the card to be returned, the money to be given out and a receipt to be printed.

(d) (i) A Personal Identification Number.
   (ii) A PIN is used to ensure the person using a bank card is entitled to use it.

(e) Any reasonable points, for example: *France – advantage*: provided only the person entitled to use the bank card knows the PIN number, this method is less susceptible to fraud. *France – disadvantage*: supermarkets have to have additional key pads for customers to type in their PINs. *UK – advantage*: it is more difficult for a casual observer to learn how to forge a customer's signature. In France, as typing in the PIN is done at a checkout, it is quite easy to see what number a customer is typing in. *UK – disadvantage*: a criminal who stole a bank card could practise forging the owner's signature.

Question 3

(a) Any reasonable answer, for example:
   – The form has a heading and a preamble explaining its purpose.
   – The form requests and has space to enter the member's name and address.
   – The subscription required and charges payable are shown.
   – Boxes are used for filling in appropriate parts of the form, e.g. the member's name.
   – Tick lists are used for filling in appropriate parts of the form, e.g. the membership category.
   – There is space to sign and date the form.

(b) – It is faster to enter a bar code than type in the member's name.
  – The shop needs to know who has borrowed their videos.
  – The membership card identifies the member.

(c) (i) The bar code on the membership card, and the bar code on each video to be borrowed.

  (ii) The bar code on each video that has been borrowed.

  (iii) As the IT system must link the member's identification number in the bar code on the membership card with the bar codes on each video borrowed, it is only necessary to input one or the other to release the link. As the member may return some but not all of the videos borrowed, it is the bar codes on these that must be input.

Question 4

(a) The purpose of verification is to make sure that what is entered into the computer is entered accurately.

(b) The **double entry** method is commonly used to verify information input using a keyboard, and it will detect transcription errors. Typically, the information written on a form is typed into the computer twice by different people. The computer checks that they have both entered the same information. If they have not, a mistake has been made and this must be corrected.

(c) Validation is carried out to see if it is reasonable to assume that the information entered is accurate.

(d) (i) Any reasonable answer, for example: if the date was the date of birth of a school pupil, in 1997 it would be reasonable to check that YY was greater than 77 and less than 92.

  (ii) Any reasonable answer, for example: legacy systems may either mistakenly treat 00 (the year 2000) as less than 99 (1999) or not recognize it as a valid date.

(e) So that it is in the same order as the old master file. This speeds up processing.

(f) (i) Update means bring up-to-date.

  (ii) Any reasonable answer, for example: *amend an employee's record*, for example, change their address; *delete an employee's record*, for example, when an employee leaves the company; *insert an employee's record*, for example, when an employee joins the company.

  (iii) Any reasonable answer, for example: the number of hours an employee has worked is calculated from the clock cards; the rate of pay is retrieved from the old master file; gross pay is calculated from hours worked multiplied by rate of pay; net pay is calculated using the details of tax and national insurance to be deducted which are also retrieved from the old master file.

  (iv) Any reasonable answer, for example:

Figure A5.1

RADIO U.K. LTD. ⚓		
Name: A. Jones	Employee number: 86502	Date: 10/07/97
Hours worked: 45	Hourly rate of pay: £3.50	
Gross pay: £157.50		
Tax: £26.25	Tax paid this year: £240.75	
National insurance: £17.40	National insurance paid this year: £136.14	
Net pay: £113.85		

(g) Any reasonable answer, for example: the master file could be backed up by keeping previous copies of it, and the transaction files used to update them. Three copies are usually kept and these are generated as the IT system is run. This is the ancestral system, with the grandfather, father and son copies.

(h) Any reasonable answer, for example: as there is often a week or more to complete payroll processing, all the information to be processed can be assembled before processing begins. In a company with a large number of employees, the information will be processed in batches to make it more controllable.

Question 5

(a) Any reasonable answer, for example: to produce posters to advertise the sports centre's programme of activities; to keep a record of payments and receipts; to produce letters to remind members that their subscriptions are overdue.

(b) Systems investigation; feasibility study; system analysis and design; program design, coding and testing; implementation; evaluation; maintenance.

(c) Systems investigation; feasibility study; implementation.

(d) Any reasonable answer, for example: a parallel run involves running the old manual system and the new IT system at the same time; the results produced by the new system are checked against the old system.

Question 6

(a) – The orders are processed overnight.
   – The orders are processed in batches.
   – Order processing is not interactive.

(b) (i) Quantity of each item ordered; customer number; invoice number.
   (ii) Customer number; customer's name; customer's address.

(c) Customer file; invoice file; customer number.

(d) Any reasonable answer, for example: the information on the invoice file could be different for every order from a customer, whereas the information on the customer file changes very infrequently. The information is separated into two files so that it is not necessary to type in all the information about a customer every time an order is placed.

Question 7

(a) – Different road routes from one place to another, showing the cost and time it would take to travel.
   – The number and location of burglaries occurring between 11.00 p.m. and 1.00 a.m.
   – The location and size of all the secondary schools in an area.

(b) (i) Any reasonable answer, for example: the police could look at patterns of burglary and try to locate the burglar's home.
   (ii) Any reasonable answer, for example: the ambulance service could predict where and when ambulances would be needed.
   (iii) Any reasonable answer, for example: a company selling lawn mowers would know in which areas it was most effective to advertise its products.
   (iv) Any reasonable answer, for example: a supermarket could consider opening a new branch in an area where people could not easily get to the shops.

(c) Any reasonable answer, for example: a GPS with a GIS could tell drivers where they are and how to get to their destinations. This would save drivers' time and the company money; the company would know exactly where its vehicles were, and could prevent misuse of them.

(d) Any reasonable answer, for example: as there would be no detailed maps of the area, it would be difficult to describe where the geologist is, and this would not help him/her find oil.

Question 8

(a) Any reasonable answer, for example: customers can book and have their booking immediately confirmed at their local ticket agency; seats will not be doubled booked.

(b) Any reasonable answer, for example: the computer system can easily be customized to show whatever seating arrangements are needed; costs could be reduced by moving administration of the booking process from the theatres to the booking agents.

(c) (i) Any reasonable answer, for example: each ticket agent will have their own user identification number and password.

 (ii) Any reasonable answer, for example: if the files are lost on the first hard disk, the fingerprint files are immediately available.

 (iii) Any reasonable answer, for example: if the main computer breaks down, the hot standby is available.

(d) (i) When many users are connected to, and in simultaneous communication with, a single computer using terminals, this is multiaccess computing.

 (ii) Real time processing is the processing of input data so quickly that when more data is input the results of the processing are already available.

 (iii) Any reasonable answer, for example: as all the ticket agents will need access from different locations, a multiaccess system is essential; real time processing is necessary to prevent double booking as many ticket agents may try to book the same seats at the same time.

Question 9 – Student answer

(a) The number printed under the bar code is also stored in the bar code.
Every member has a different number on their membership card.
Bar codes can be read into the computer without the need for data preparation.

 Examiner's note Correct.

(b) (i) It is faster.

 Examiner's note Too vague. What is faster and why? A bar code reader will input a bar code faster and more accurately than is possible by typing it in.

 (ii) The librarian types the number because the bar code reader is broken.

 Examiner's note Correct.

(c) (i) When you work out the check digit on a bar code you should always get the same answer.
Every bar code has a different check digit.

 Examiner's note The first answer is correct but the second is incorrect. Many bar codes have the same check digit. The check digit does not identify a book, it helps check that the bar code has been read correctly.

 (ii) When a bar code is read its check digit is worked out. This should be the same as the one on the bar code. If it isn't then the bar code hasn't been read accurately.

 Examiner's note Correct.

(d) (i) So that the computer will know what they are.

 Examiner's note This is too vague. Both bar codes are read so that the computer can record the borrower, the book borrowed and the connection between them.

 (ii) Because the computer remembers and does not need it.

 Examiner's note Possibly, but this is not well expressed. The connection between the borrower and the book borrowed has been recorded by the computer. Reading the book's bar code can release this connection, as it is possible that each book has a unique bar code.

(e) (i) Multitasking is when one person is running more than one program at the same time.

Examiner's note Almost correct. The student has forgotten to mention that this is happening on one computer.

(ii) This is a lot of people on different network computers all using the same mainframe computer.

Examiner's note Correct. The answer could be improved by mentioning the network connections.

Question 10 – Student answer

(a) (i) Employee number.

Examiner's note Correct.

(ii) Because it will be needed.

Examiner's note Too vague. The employee number is unique and is needed on both files so that an employee's record on each file can be matched.

(iii) Bank account number.
Pay rate.
Total pay to date.
Tax code.

Examiner's note Correct. Assuming that the question refers only to normal transactions in relation to pay, only employee number and the hours worked would not be in the master file.

(b) It could make sure that the 'hours worked this month' is less than a sensible number of hours.

Examiner's note This is correct. However, a better answer would use technical language more effectively. The system could do a range check to make sure that, for example, 0 < 'hours worked this month' < 280.

(c) (i) Sequential access.

Examiner's note Correct. Batch processing could use any type of file access but in this context only sequential or direct access would be appropriate.

(ii) Make a copy of the files.

Examiner's note This is correct but lacks detail. The need for multiple copies and some way of organizing these should be noted, for example, the ancestral system. The need to keep both master and transaction files should also be mentioned.

(d) (i) So that if someone gets it they don't know what it is.

Examiner's note This is essentially correct but too vague. A better answer would note that if an unauthorized person accessed the data during transmission they would not be able to understand it as they would not know how to decode it.

(ii) The amount.

Examiner's note Correct, but the bank would also need to know an employee's account number.

6 Solutions
IT, hardware and software, operating systems and networks

★ SOLUTIONS TO REVISION ACTIVITIES

Question 1

(a)

a monitor	hardware
a wordprocessor	software
a printer	hardware
a mouse	hardware
a database	software
a modem	hardware

(b) Hard disk; monitor; keyboard.

Question 2

(a) A CD-ROM drive; stereo speakers; 32 Mbyte, 2.4 Gbyte; processor box.

(b)

a monitor	output
keyboard	input
speaker	output
a mouse	input
scanner	input
a printer	output

Question 3

(a) Hard disk; floppy disk; CD-ROM.
(b) Save; delete; update.

Question 4

(a) OMR; bar codes; Magnetic Ink Character Recognition (MICR).
(b) – Information can be output from a PC using a monitor, a printer or speakers.
    – A printer buffer is RAM memory built into a printer.
    – Graph plotters are used to output high quality line drawings on large sheets of paper.

Question 5

(a) Supervise programs; support multitasking; format a floppy disk.
(b) – Backup files regularly.
    – Use firewalls to prevent access from external networks.
    – Use User Identification Numbers and passwords.

SOLUTIONS TO PRACTICE QUESTIONS

Question 1

(a) – A database is computer software.
 – A printer is a hardware device.
 – Information Technology is the use of computers and other equipment to store, process and transmit information.

(b) A desk top PC; Random Access Memory; backing storage; backing storage.

(c) (i) A file can be stored on backing storage. It may contain programs or data.
 (ii) A directory is a list of all the files on a disk. It is also known as a catalogue.
 (iii) When a file is loaded it is retrieved from backing storage and stored in the computer's memory.
 (iv) When a file is renamed, its filename is changed.
 (v) When a file is copied, another copy of it is made on backing storage.
 (vi) When two or more files are merged, they are made into one file.

Question 2

(a) Any reasonable answer, for example: keyboard, mouse, scanner.

(b) Any reasonable answer, for example: monitor, printer, speaker.

(c) (i) Any reasonable answer, for example: a joystick used to play a computer game.
 (ii) Any reasonable answer, for example: use OMR to buy a national lottery ticket.
 (iii) Any reasonable answer, for example: OCR software is used when a book is scanned into a computer in a form that can be input to a wordprocessor.
 (iv) Any reasonable answer, for example: Kimball tags are used in some clothes shops to record sales.
 (v) Any reasonable answer, for example: magnetic stripe cards are used as bank cards.
 (vi) Any reasonable answer, for example: bar codes are used in supermarkets to identify goods being sold.
 (vii) Any reasonable answer, for example: a touch screen could be used by a Tourist Information Centre to give the public easy access to its accommodation database.

(d) (i) Any reasonable answer, for example: see Figure 6.3, p. 63.
 (ii) The cheque number; customer account number; the bank sort code.
 (iii) The amount.

Question 3

(a) Voice recognition is the input and recognition of spoken words by a computer. A suitable input device is a microphone.

(b) Any reasonable answer, for example: a disabled person could operate a computer using voice recognition.

(c) Speech synthesis is a series of sounds generated by a computer which mimic human speech. A suitable output device is a speaker.

(d) Any reasonable answer, for example: an on-board computer in a car could talk to the driver using speech synthesis so that the driver could keep his/her eyes on the road.

(e) Any reasonable answer, for example: less demand for session musicians as different instruments can be generated by IT; high quality performance is not necessary as mistakes can be corrected later.

Question 4

(a) Desk Top Publishing (DTP).

(b) Any reasonable answer, for example: you can easily layout the page in columns; you can import and re-size pictures and other graphics; you can use a master page to define a consistent page layout.

(c) Scanner; input; edit; cut and paste.

(d) Video digitizer; digital camera; clip art library.

(e) Wordprocessing; OCR scanning; e-mail message.

Question 5

(a) – Spooling is the queuing of files waiting to be printed on a hard disk.
   – Using printer buffers or spooling releases the computer so that it can continue with other tasks.
   – A printer buffer is RAM memory built into a printer.

(b) Any reasonable answer, for example: they are cheap to buy and run; they are reliable and robust in operation; they produce carbon copies.

Question 6

(a) (i) A window is a rectangular subdivision of the screen which enables the user to look at the output from a program.

   (ii) An icon is a picture that represents a command, function, process, device or tool.

   (iii) A menu is a list of tasks which can be carried out by a computer program. The user selects a task from the menu.

   (iv) A pointer is an arrow or similar symbol which appears on the monitor screen. Its form depends on the operation being used. The position of the pointer is controlled by the mouse (it is the on-screen representation of the mouse.)

(b) Any reasonable answer, for example: selecting an operation using a GUI is less error prone than typing in text OS commands; with text OS commands before you start you need to know what it is you want to do, whereas with a GUI what you can do is visible on the screen.

(c) Sharing; multiaccess; multitasking.

(d) Any reasonable answer, for example: manage printer queues and spooling; organize User Identification Numbers and Passwords; keep a log of network users.

Question 7

(a) A Local Area Network (LAN) is a small network, probably in one room or a building. The Internet is an international network made up of smaller, interconnected networks. A Wide Area Network (WAN) is a national or international network.

(b) Any reasonable answer, for example: the electronic yellow pages; the national railway timetable; information about the British Royal Family.

Question 8

(a) Any reasonable answer, for example: see Figure 6.5, p. 65.

(b) (i) A fileserver is a computer attached to a network whose main function is to enable network stations to access shared files stored on one or more hard disks that are accessible over the network.

   (ii) A LAN is a network with permanent links between all hardware connected to the network. Many LANs are located in one room or in a single building.

   (iii) A WAN is a network spread over a wide area, possibly international, making use of both permanent cable connections and temporary connections using the telephone network.

(c) (i) Any reasonable answer, for example: pupils can use their work on compatible computers not attached to the network.

   (ii) Any reasonable answer, for example: pupils' work is not taking up space on the fileserver's hard disk, giving more room to store software for use in school.

   (iii) Any reasonable answer, for example: they will not need to remember to have their floppy disks with them when they use IT in school.

   (iv) Any reasonable answer, for example: pupils' IT coursework will not get lost (provided regular backups are made!).

(d) (i) Any reasonable answer, for example: *Advantage*: dot matrix printers are cheap to run, reliable and robust. *Disadvantage*: dot matrix printers print much slower.

(ii) Any reasonable answer, for example: *Advantage*: laser printers produce much better quality printout. *Disadvantage*: laser printers are expensive to buy and run.
(e) Any reasonable answer, for example: *Problem*: pupils could access each others' work and change it. *Solution*: give pupils their own User Identification Numbers and passwords. *Problem*: some pupils might put IT equipment in their bags and steal it. *Solution*: connect all IT equipment to an alarm system that is always switched on.

Question 9 – Student answer
(a) (i) A; C; E.

Examiner's note Correct.

(ii) A; F; D.

Examiner's note A and F are correct. Although D is backing storage, it will be ignored as information can be input to a computer from backing storage.

(iii) E; C.

Examiner's note Correct.

(b) D.

Examiner's note Incorrect. D points at the floppy disk drive. B points at the processor box where the network card will be installed.

(c) (i) To stop people getting into the computer.

Examiner's note Too vague. The student has not distinguished clearly between authorized and unauthorized users. Passwords prevent unauthorized access; they do not stop authorized use of the computer.

(ii) So that if someone gets to know the password they cannot use the computer.

Examiner's note Too vague. If someone gets to know the password they will be able to use the computer, but not for long if the password is changed frequently!

(iii) To make sure that the new password has been input accurately.

Examiner's note Correct.

(d) (i) Is the information code 1, 2 or 3?

Examiner's note Correct.

(ii) (Draws line from B to Start.)

Examiner's note Incorrect. The line should re-join the flowchart just before the information code is input.

Question 10 – Student answer
(a) Software that uses text, sound, pictures, music and video on a computer.

Examiner's note Correct.

(b) (i) They could load it on the computer and look at it.

Examiner's note This is true but far too vague. The answer needs to refer to the possibility of accessing data on CD-ROM using search conditions similar to those used to search a database. An example would be helpful.

(ii) Advantage to customer: customers can find what they want within their price range more quickly and easily.
Advantage to sports firm: it is much cheaper to send out a large catalogue on a CD-ROM than printed on paper.

Examiner's note Advantage to customer and sports firm: correct.

(c) The computer could be used to print specialist catalogues that could be sent to those customers who are interested.

> **Examiner's note** Incorrect. Preparing and sending out brief specialist catalogues only to those customers who are interested would be a useful feature of the system. However, this does not answer the question as it does not use the multimedia facilities of the computer.

7 Solutions
Social implications

SOLUTIONS TO REVISION ACTIVITIES

Question 1
(a) – Computer programmers and systems analysts are in great demand as companies install IT systems.
  – There are fewer watchmakers who can build and repair mechanical watches.
  – Checkout operators do not need quick, accurate mental arithmetic as automatic tills can add up customers' bills and calculate the change required faster and more accurately.
(b) Secretary; policeman; bank clerk.

Question 2
(a) Searched; improved.
(b) – Personal information must be kept accurate and up-to-date.
  – Anyone who asks must be told what information is kept about them, and allowed to change it if it is incorrect.
  – Personal information should only be kept as long as it is needed.

Question 3
(a) Stripe cards; CCTV; electronic tag.
(b) – Stripe card operated entrances could register pupils and prevent unauthorized people getting into schools.
  – IT systems on motorways can identify cars that are speeding and fine their owners automatically.
  – Criminals can have electronic tags fitted so that if they move outside their homes the police are informed.

Question 4
(a) Security alarm system; video recorder; washing machine.
(b)

Older washing machines had hand-operated agitators and wringers. In a modern machine these are automatically controlled by a built-in program.	*true*
It is more convenient to go to the nearest bank during opening hours than to use telephone banking from home.	*false*
You can only purchase virtual goods in a virtual shopping mall.	*false*
Cable companies provide TV, and offer a range of other services, including telephone and Internet access.	*true*
Access to e-mail from home is useful for teleworkers.	*true*
Using a bank card, you can obtain foreign currency from cashpoints in Europe.	*true*

Question 5
(a) Essential; teleworking; regulated.
(b) Fibre optic cables; e-mail; cheap PCs.

SOLUTIONS TO PRACTICE QUESTIONS

Question 1
(a) E-mail connection; industry standard software; laser printer.
(b) Speakers; CD-ROM; joystick.
(c) Any reasonable answer, for example: see Figure 6.1 on p. 62.
(d) Any reasonable answer, for example: *Advantage*: teleworkers do not have to commute, saving time and money. *Disadvantage*: teleworkers may feel isolated as they cannot meet friends at work.

Question 2
(a) Any reasonable answer, for example: name; emergency telephone number; doctor address; form.
(b) – Give pupils a copy of their own personal information and ask them to check it.
    – Send parents a copy of the personal information about their children that the school has recorded and ask them to check it.
    – Ask a teacher to interview pupils in private and check that what has been stored is correct.
(c) Any reasonable answer, for example: *Problem*: pupils could access teachers' personal information and change it. *Solution*: give pupils' restricted permissions so that they can access only a part of the information on the network. *Problem*: some pupils might hack into the parts of the network that they have been denied access to. *Solution*: keep a log of users and their activities so that illegal access can be traced.

Question 3
(a) (i)   Any reasonable answer, for example: an infra red beam is bounced off a car as it moves towards a receptor; this is repeated at a fixed time interval. The computer knows how quickly the second beam should return to the receptor if the car is travelling below the speed limit. If the car is not travelling below the speed limit a digital camera photographs its number plate. This photograph is scanned using OCR, and the car registration number used to search a database, find the owner's address, and send him/her notice of a fine.
    (ii) Any reasonable answer, for example: the roads are safer as more drivers obey the speed limits.
    (iii) Any reasonable answer, for example: they have to pay a fine if they go too fast.
(b) (i)   Any reasonable answer, for example: as cars enter and leave the motorway a device built into them transmits their registration numbers to a receiver. Cars' registration numbers are used to retrieve their owners' names and addresses from a database, and they are automatically billed.
    (ii) Any reasonable answer, for example: there could be fewer cars on motorways as charges will encourage people to travel in other ways; motorways could be maintained to a higher standard as users pay for them directly.
    (iii) Any reasonable answer, for example: drivers have to pay every time they use a motorway; drivers may have to use A roads instead of motorways as they cannot afford the charges.
(c) (i)   Any reasonable answer, for example: there is less money on the premises so there is less likelihood they will be robbed.
    (ii) Any reasonable answer, for example: company drivers do not have to spend their own money on petrol, as it can be charged direct to their employer's credit account.
    (iii) Any reasonable answer, for example: it takes longer to pay using a credit card so drivers may have to queue longer.
(d) (i)   Any reasonable answer, for example: if a car is stolen, the police could find it faster.
    (ii) Any reasonable answer, for example: a driver's privacy could be threatened.

Question 4

(a) (i) PC, modem, subscription to an ISP, browser, telephone line.

    (ii) Any reasonable answer, for example: courses available at universities throughout the world, including Huddersfield University; library catalogues.

    (iii) Any reasonable answer, for example: you could use a search engine; you surf the WWW until you have found the information required.

(b) (i) Any reasonable answer, for example: on-line shopping is using a PC to connect to a WWW information server that has information about goods for sale, and purchasing them.

    (ii) Any reasonable answer, for example: you do not have to travel to the shops and goods are delivered to your door; a wider variety of goods are available at very low prices.

    (iii) Any reasonable answer, for example: you cannot judge the quality of the goods as you can only see their image on the screen; you have to wait for the goods to be delivered.

(c) (i) Any reasonable answer, for example: transfer money from one account to another; see a statement of transactions on your account.

    (ii) Any reasonable answer, for example: you can access your account from home; you can access your account at any time of the day or night.

    (iii) Any reasonable answer, for example: you have to have a PC and a modem, etc. to access your bank account; on-line transactions on the WWW are not secure, so someone might find out how to access your account and take your money.

(d) (i) Any reasonable answer, for example: pornography; information about religious cults.

    (ii) Any reasonable answer, for example: they might be concerned that their children or pupils could access information that would hurt or upset them.

    (iii) Any reasonable answer, for example: you could use firewall software that blocks access to particular WWW information servers or blocks information containing specified key words.

Question 5

(a) Any reasonable answer, for example: withdrawing money from cashpoints.

(b) Any reasonable answer, for example: *Advantage*: customers can withdraw money all day, every day. *Disadvantage*: if a cashpoint retains your cash card, you cannot withdraw money until the bank sends you another one. This could be inconvenient.

(c) Any reasonable answer, for example: bank clerks perform fewer routine transactions and focus more on service to customers.

(d) Any reasonable answer, for example: the introduction of EFTPOS means that goods can be paid for direct from a customer's bank account. Shop assistants handle less cash and must know how to handle stripe card payments.

(e) Any reasonable answer, for example: shops handle less cash so they are less likely to be robbed.

Question 6

(a) (i) Any reasonable answer, for example: it is difficult to be sure whether IT has led to overall losses or gains in the total number of people employed, for example, there are fewer people employed in bank branches but there are many more employed in telephone banking which depends heavily on IT.

    (ii) Any reasonable answer, for example: more people need IT skills to find a job.

    (iii) Any reasonable answer, for example: IT can do some dirty and dangerous jobs, such as welding, so people do not have poor working conditions.

    (iv) Any reasonable answer, for example: IT increases workers' productivity, for example, secretaries can use mail merge to produce personalized letters to customers instead of having to type them all out individually.

(b) (i) Any reasonable answer, for example: robots are more consistent and produce better quality work when doing repetitive work on production lines, for example, welding car bodies; robots can operate more effectively in dangerous environments where people may be injured, for example, spraying car bodies with toxic, inflammable paint.

   (ii) Any reasonable answer, for example: people are more flexible and will work in restricted areas that robots cannot easily access. People are better at adding individual touches, such as, customized body stripes.

(c) File sharing; e-mail; networks.

(d) Any reasonable answer, for example: the 'haves' will have access to more employment opportunities; the 'have nots' will not; the 'haves' will have access to information which could help them improve their income and lifestyles; the 'have nots' will not; the 'have nots' will be increasingly dependant on social welfare; the 'haves' will have less need for the welfare state.

Question 7

(a) Any reasonable answer, for example: an electronic tag is fixed to a criminal and they are told not to leave their homes. If they do, the IT system detects this and action is taken. They could be automatically fined or their period of restraint extended, or the police are sent to arrest them.

(b) Any reasonable answer, for example: criminals may find a way of removing their tag or otherwise disabling the IT system; if a criminal is not concerned about the consequences of moving outside the imposed limits then tags have no restraining effect whatsoever.

(c) Any reasonable answer, for example: the cost to society of imprisoning criminals at home could be much less than keeping them in purpose-built prisons.

(d) Any reasonable answer, for example: if the criminal had been convicted for stealing from his/her neighbours, it might not resolve the problem if the criminal was sentenced to remain at home.

Question 8

(a) Any reasonable answer, for example: in a real village people live close together. In the 'global village' people seem to live close together because they can communicate with each other using IT as easily as people in a real village can communicate. This is possible because of the development of global networks and communications software, such as e-mail.

(b) Any reasonable answer, for example: some jobs or parts of them can be done entirely using IT, for example, preparing a newspaper for publishing. Consequently, they can be done anywhere in the world. This means that workers in these jobs are competing for employment with workers throughout the world. This is possible because of the development of global IT networks and communications software. As the UK has an educated population and good access to the global IT networks it is well placed to attract these types of employment.

(c) Any reasonable answer, for example: if a computer cannot communicate with other types of computers it will not be able to communicate with all the computers connected to the global network. This means that some users will not be able to communicate with or work with some other users.

(d) Any reasonable answer, for example: *For*: connection to EC networks will give us access to more opportunities for employment and large markets for our goods and services; harmonization of networking standards, employment practices; social welfare and currency will ensure that the whole EC can benefit from these new opportunities. *Against*: connection to the global network gives us access to global markets which are much larger than those of the EC, and there are correspondingly greater employment opportunities. We do not need a close relationship with the EC to benefit. Harmonization of EC employment practices and social welfare is irrelevant in a global context. Our currency and language are known and valued throughout the world, whereas those of many countries in the EC are not.

Question 9 – Student answer

(a) Bank account number.

> ***Examiner's note*** Correct.

(b) Field; sequential.

> ***Examiner's note*** Field is correct. Sequential is incorrect. A unique customer number would be used as a key field.

(c) A Local Area Network connects the computers within a branch of the bank. A Wide Area Network connects the computers at a branch of the bank to the computer in Swindon.

> ***Examiner's note*** Correct.

(d) (i) You put the card in the cashpoint, type in your PIN and get your money.

> ***Examiner's note*** Correct but vague. The student has forgotten that it will be necessary to tell the cashpoint how much money is needed, and has not mentioned that the card will be returned or a receipt printed.

(ii) Customers can get money when they want.

> ***Examiner's note*** Correct but the student should mention at least one more way in which the introduction of ATMs has changed the lifestyle of customers.

Question 10 – Student answer

(a) Right 1: You don't have to give anyone your information.
   Right 2: You can ask to see your personal information.
   Right 3: You can correct it if it is wrong.

> ***Examiner's note*** Right 1 is incorrect as there are occasions when individuals are required to give others information about themselves, for example, to the police. In addition, it is not a part of the Data Protection Act. Rights 2 and 3 are correct.

(b) Precaution 1: Backup data regularly.
   Precaution 2: Use User Identification Numbers and Passwords.
   Precaution 3: Keep all your data on a floppy disk.

> ***Examiner's note*** Precautions 1 and 2 are correct. Precaution 3 could contradict Precaution 1 and it will probably make it more likely that data is lost!

Grading

Grade descriptions are provided by SCAA in its publication *GCSE Regulations and Criteria*. They apply to all GCSE syllabuses although those that appear in a particular examination board's syllabuses may have been slightly modified.

Grade descriptions give a general idea of the standard you will have to achieve to be awarded a particular grade. They take into account your performance in both the written examinations and the coursework. The grade awarded will depend on the extent to which you have met the overall assessment objectives. Your lack of skills, knowledge and understanding in some areas could be balanced by better performance in others.

Grade descriptions

The following grade descriptions have been adapted from those given by SCAA, and will give you an indication of what you have to know, understand and do to be awarded a particular grade.

Grade F

You show a basic knowledge and understanding of familiar, simple IT applications, and the techniques, hardware and software used. You know some basic terms and definitions, and know when to use IT. When you collect information, you know that questions must be carefully framed. You can use IT to present your work and can show how you would use it to develop and modify your ideas. You can edit, manipulate and search information. You can develop, test and modify instructions to control hardware devices. You can use computer models and simulations to detect and explore patterns and relationships.

Grade C

You show knowledge and understanding of the range and scope of IT applications, and of the techniques and systems used, including the software and hardware. You have a good grasp of basic terms and definitions, and can contrast and compare related ideas. You know when to use IT, and can analyse, design and evaluate IT systems. You can use information from a wide range of sources to produce IT-based solutions to a range of problems, and can test hypotheses. You can develop, test and improve programs that control hardware devices showing awareness of the need for efficiency and economy. You know that hardware devices can be made to respond to data input from sensors. You can use computer models to help make and test hypotheses. You show a clear sense of audience and purpose when you make presentations.

Grade A

You show a sound knowledge and understanding of the range and scope of IT applications, and of the techniques and systems used, including the software and hardware. Some of these IT applications will be outside your everyday experience. You have a good grasp of terms and definitions, and can contrast and compare related ideas. You know when to use IT, and can apply general principles to particular situations and can illustrate these using examples. You can also analyse, design and evaluate IT systems. You can evaluate software packages and complex computer models, and analyse the situation for which they were developed and assess their efficiency, appropriateness and ease of use. You can design and implement IT systems for others to use. You know how to prevent the loss or corruption of information stored on IT systems, and can describe what should be done to avoid personal information being misused. You can produce effective, working IT systems to solve a range of practical problems of varying complexity.

Timed practice papers

PRACTICE PAPER 1 – FOUNDATION LEVEL

You should complete this paper in 1 hour.

Question 1

(a) Tick **three** boxes to show those tasks that are easier using graphics software.   [*3*]

	Tick three boxes
Drawing on handmade paper of varying non-standard sizes.	
Copying part of a picture several times within the picture.	
Sketching a landscape from the summit of a mountain.	
Using textiles, grasses and twigs to introduce a variety of textures.	
Colouring in evenly.	
Making several good copies of the finished picture.	

(b) (i) Explain what is meant by clip art.   [*2*]
    (ii) Write down one advantage and one disadvantage of using clip art.   [*2*]
    (iii) Using words from the list, complete the sentences: [*3*]

   bigger   cut and paste   export   import   palette   scroll   smaller

   – Font size 22 is .... than font size 14.
   – To move an image you can use the .... feature.
   – A .... shows you the range of colours available.

(c) State two other ways pictures, photographs and other images can be input to a computer.   [*2*]

Total 12 marks

Question 2

A local newsagent keeps information about customers on a database.

(a) Tick **three** boxes to show which of these statements is most likely to be true.   [*3*]

	Tick three boxes
A newsagent would not use database software as data logging software would be more useful.	
A database would give better results as it is more fashionable.	
A newsagent may not use database software as there may be too few customers to justify the expense of using IT.	
The newsagent could use a database to print a list of all those customers who have the *Daily Mirror* delivered on a Thursday.	
The newsagent would need a modem to access the database.	
The information in the database would have to be kept up-to-date or customers could be charged the wrong amount.	

(b) Tick **three** boxes to show which of these statements is most likely to be true.   [*3*]

	Tick three boxes
There will be several fields in a record.	
There is one record for each customer.	
There is one file for each customer.	
There will be several animals in a field.	
There is one field for each customer.	
The fields will be in the same order in every record.	

(c) Tick **two** boxes to show which of these statements is most likely to be true.   [*2*]

	Tick two boxes
Fields are coded so that they use up less space on backing storage.	
Coded data cannot be stolen by hackers.	
Codes are fun to use.	
Codes should be long and difficult to understand.	
Codes should be short but easy to understand.	

(d) Design a form for new customers to fill in.   [*4*]

Total 12 marks

Question 3

A farmer delivers milk and yoghurt door-to-door. The farmer keeps records of deliveries to customers using a spreadsheet. This is a part of the spreadsheet showing sales to one customer during one week.

	A	B	C
1	Customer: Mr Jones, 121 Thornton Road.		
2		Milk (litre)	Yogurt (carton)
3	Monday	1	2
4	Tuesday	2	1
5	Wednesday	1	2
6	Thursday	2	1
7	Friday	1	1
8	Saturday	4	3
9	Total	11	10
10	Unit price	£0.61	£0.52
11	Total to collect	£11.91	

(a) Write down the cell reference of a cell that could contain:
  (i) Text. [1]
  (ii) Numbers. [1]
(b) Write down the formulae that would be in these cells:
  (i) B9. [1]
  (ii) B11. [1]
(c) Describe **one** advantage in using formulae in a spreadsheet. [1]
(d) Mr Jones orders more milk and yoghurt on Saturday than on other days. Give a reasonable explanation for this. [1]
(e) Describe **two** possible effects if the information the farmer entered into the spreadsheet was incorrect. [2]
(f) Before the farmer recorded deliveries using a spreadsheet, this information was written down in a notebook.
  (i) Give **two** advantages in using a spreadsheet. [2]
  (ii) Give **two** disadvantages in using a spreadsheet. [2]

Total 12 marks

Question 4

A computer-controlled robot is used to cut holes in steel panels. The robot has a cutter attached to it.

These are the commands that control the robot. You can change the number of units moved.

Command	Meaning of command
LEFT 5	Move the cutter left 5 units
RIGHT 1	Move the cutter right 1 unit
UP 4	Move the cutter up 4 units
DOWN 3	Move the cutter down 3 units
CUT ON	Start cutting
CUT OFF	Stop cutting

(a) Complete these commands to make the robot cut out a square. [1]

    CUT ON
    UP 3
    RIGHT 3
    ....
    LEFT 3
    CUT OFF

(b) Write the commands that make the robot cut out the shaded part. The cutter starts at HOME and should be returned to HOME. [5]

Figure TP.1

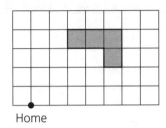

Home

(c) Using words from the list, complete the sentence. [1]
    food processing   batch processing   real time processing   multiaccess   e-mail

The computer that controls the robot must run the commands using

....

(d) The cutter can overheat and damage the robot.
    (i) Explain how the computer can know how hot the cutter is. [1]
    (ii) In this context, explain what is meant by feedback. [4]
    Total 12 marks

Question 5
(a) This is a drawing of a desk top computer.

Figure TP.2

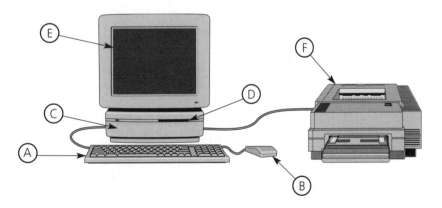

    (i)   Write down the labels of **two** parts of the computer that can be used for input only. [2]
    (ii) Write down the labels of **two** parts of the computer that can be used for output only. [2]
    (iii) Write down the label of **one** part of the computer that can be used for backing storage. [1]
(b) A floppy disk can store 1.14 Megabytes. Approximately how many characters can be stored on a floppy disk? [1]
(c) The computer has this software. [1]
    Desk top publishing (DTP)   Logo   games   e-mail   operating system

When the computer is switched on it runs some software first. From the list, write down the name of the software the computer runs first.

(d) The computer can run wordprocessing software.

   (i)   The computer is switched on. Describe how you would run the wordprocessing software.   *[1]*

   (ii) Describe how you would save a wordprocessing document on a floppy disk.   *[2]*

   (iii) Give two advantages in saving wordprocessing documents on floppy disk.   *[2]*

Total 12 marks

PRACTICE PAPER 2 – HIGHER LEVEL

You should complete this paper in 1 hour.

Question 1

The personnel department in a mail order company keeps a database of information about all the company's employees.
This is a part of the database:

Family_Name	First_Name	Employee_Number	Sex	Job_Description	Pay (£)
Nelson	Joan	2342	F	packer	145
Afzal	Shakeel	2392	M	electrician	180
Watson	Trevor	0045	M	driver	175
Houseman	Linda	2342	F	driver	175
Battye	Lorraine	0167	F	packer	145
McFee	Alison	0774	F	packer	145
Malik	Rizwan	0997	M	electrician	180

(a) How many records are shown?   *[1]*

(b) How many fields are shown?   *[1]*

(c) Linda Houseman's Employee_Number is incorrect.

   (i)   Explain why her Employee_Number cannot be correct.   *[1]*

   (ii) Write down an Employee_Number that might be correct.   *[1]*

   (iii) Which field would be used as the key field?   *[1]*

   (iv) Explain why key fields are used.   *[1]*

(d) Using words from the list, complete the sentences.   *[3]*

     apportioned   inserted   reduced   amended   deleted   totalled

    – Alison McFee has left the company. Her record will have to be ....

    – Anita Spedding starts work on Monday. A new record will have to be ....

    – Joan Nelson has been promoted to supervisor. Her Job_Description will have to be ....

(e) (i)   Describe one possible effect if the information stored on the database was incorrect.   *[1]*

   (ii) Give a validation check for the Sex field.   *[1]*

   (iii) Describe one way the personnel department could find out if the information stored on the database is correct. The way you describe must comply with the Data Protection Act.   *[1]*

Total 12 marks

Question 2

A roofing contractor uses a spreadsheet to work out the cost of replacing a slate roof.

	A	B	C	D
1	**Mr Johnston, 27 Low Fold, HD3 5BN – quote for replacing slate roof**			
2		**materials**	**labour**	
3	scaffolding	£200.00	£50.00	
4	strip roof		£250.00	
5	clean spars and treat	£100.00	£75.00	
6	fit lathes and underslaters felt	£250.00	£150.00	
7	fit lead flashing and slates	£1,500.00	£1,000.00	
8	re-bed ridges and point	£15.00	£50.00	
9	remove waste and tidy site		£50.00	
10	totals	£2,065.00	£1,625.00	
11	total labour and materials	£3,690.00		
12	VAT at 17.5%	£645.75		
13	total quote including VAT	£4,335.75		

(a) Write down the formula that would be in cell B10. [1]

(b) Spreadsheet cells can contain different types of information.
  – State **two** different types of information that cells can contain other than formulae.
  – Write down the cell reference of a cell that contains each type of information. [2]

(c) The contractor has over estimated the labour costs for fitting the lead flashing and slates. This is changed to £800. As a result the formulae in four other cells are re-calculated.
  – Write down the cell references of these cells. [1]

(d) (i) Give **two** advantages to the contractor in using a spreadsheet. [2]
  (ii) Give **two** disadvantages to the contractor in using a spreadsheet. [2]

(e) The contractor uses the spreadsheet to generate a bar chart showing the cost of labour. Draw this bar chart. [4]

Total 12 marks

Question 3

(a) Teletext emulators are sometimes used in Tourist Information Centres to advertise hotels, bed and breakfast, self-catering cottages and other services.
  (i) Explain what is meant by a teletext emulator. [1]
  (ii) Give **one** advantage and **one** disadvantage of using a teletext emulator to the Tourist Information Centre. [2]
  (iii) Give **one** advantage and **one** disadvantage of using a teletext emulator to the Tourist Information Centre's customers. [2]

(b) Teletext information services can be accessed using some domestic televisions. In addition, some televisions have fastext. Evaluate the effectiveness of fastext. [3]

(c) Information services are also available on the World Wide Web. Explain what is meant by the World Wide Web. [2]

(d) The World Wide Web is interactive. Give **two** advantages in access to information being interactive. [2]

Total 12 marks

Question 4

(a) At 2.00 a.m., a car approaches a set of traffic lights at the junction of two roads. The lights turn to green as the car approaches. Describe a control system that would ensure that the traffic lights turn green as the car approaches.   [2]

(b) At 9.00 a.m., high volumes of traffic approach the junction from all directions. Describe three features of a control system that could manage high volumes of traffic at the junction.   [3]

(c) The junction is a part of a ring road. The highway authorities want the control system to ensure that the traffic moves round the ring road at a steady 30 mph.

    (i)   Describe how this could be done.   [2]

    (ii)   Describe one advantage of the control system to the traffic police.   [1]

    (iii) Describe one advantage of the control system to drivers.   [1]

    (iv) Describe one benefit of the control system to the environment.   [1]

(d) Describe two other ways using IT can benefit the environment.   [3]

Total 12 marks

Question 5

A supermarket stock control system uses bar codes and laser scanners.

(a) Describe in detail how the receipt given to a customer can show the price and description of the goods purchased.   [5]

(b) Stock can be ordered automatically. Describe in detail how this can be done.   [3]

(c) Describe in detail two other tasks that a supermarket stock control system could do.   [4]

Total 12 marks

Answers

Question 1

(a) – Copying part of a picture several times within the picture.
    – Colouring in evenly.
    – Making several copies of the finished picture.   [*3*]

(b) (i) Any reasonable answer, for example: Clip art is pictures and illustrations that are available in electronic form for importing into a wordprocessor or other software.   [*2*]

    (ii) Any reasonable answer, for example: *Advantage*: high quality drawings are immediately available for use in a document. *Disadvantage*: clip art may be used by anyone and so the document is not unique.   [*2*]

    (iii) Bigger   cut and paste   palette.   [*3*]

(c) Any reasonable answer, for example: You could take a picture using a digital camera and download it into the computer. You could use a scanner to input photographs or line drawings.   [*2*]

Total 12 marks

Question 2

(a) – A newsagent may not use database software as there may be too few customers to justify the expense of using IT.
    – The newsagent could use a database to print a list of all those customers who have the *Daily Mirror* delivered on a Thursday.
    – The information in the database would have to be kept up-to-date or customers could be charged the wrong amount.   [*3*]

(b) – There will be several fields in a record.
    – There is one record for each customer.
    – The fields will be in the same order in every record.   [*3*]

(c) – Fields are coded so that they use up less space on backing storage.
    – Codes should be short but easy to understand.   [*2*]

(d) – Any reasonable answer, 1 mark each, for example:
    – The form has a heading and a preamble explaining its purpose.
    – The form has space to enter the customer's name and address.
    – The form has space to enter the customer's daily paper.
    – Boxes are used for filling in appropriate parts of the form, e.g. the customer's name.
    – Tick lists are used for filling in appropriate parts of the form, e.g. the customer's daily paper.
    – There is space to sign and date the form.   [*4*]

Total 12 marks

Question 3

(a) (i) Any reasonable answer, for example: A4.   [*1*]
    (ii) Any reasonable answer, for example: B7 (but not B9, C9 or B11).   [*1*]

(b) (i) sum(B3:B8).   [*1*]
    (ii) B9*B10+C9*C10.   [*1*]

(c) Any reasonable answer, for example: formulae are re-calculated automatically when the values of the numbers are changed.   [*1*]

(d) Any reasonable answer, for example: milk is not delivered on Sunday so Mr Jones has enough for two days delivered on Saturday. [1]
(e) Any reasonable answer, for example:
  – Mr Jones could be charged the wrong amount.
  – The farmer might deliver too much milk. [2]
(f) (i) Any reasonable answer, for example:
  – Once the spreadsheet has been set up, it is quicker for the farmer to use it than to work out all the calculations on a piece of paper.
  – The farmer can be sure the calculations are carried out accurately. [2]
  (ii) Any reasonable answer, for example:
  – The farmer must be able to use a computer and a spreadsheet.
  – The farmer must have access to a computer and a spreadsheet. [2]

Total 12 marks

Question 4
(a) DOWN 3. [1]
(b) – Starts with CUT OFF – 1 mark. [5]
  – A correct sequence to move from Home to the cut – 1 mark.
  – CUT ON before the hole is cut and CUT OFF after the hole is cut – 1 mark.
  – A correct sequence to cut the hole – 1 mark.
  – A correct sequence to move from the cut to Home – 1 mark.
(c) Real time processing. [1]
(d) (i) Any reasonable answer, for example: a heat sensor built into the cutter is connected to the computer. [1]
  – Input from heat sensor to computer – 1 mark.
  – Computer decides if the cutter is too hot – 1 mark.
  – If the cutter is too hot the computer turns it off – 1 mark.
  – The sequence is cyclical – 1 mark.

Total 12 marks

Question 5
(a) (i) A, B. [2]
  (ii) E, F. [2]
  (iii) D. [1]
(b) Any reasonable answer between 1,100,000 and 1,200,000 for example:
  – 1,140,000 approximately.
  – 1,195,376.6 exactly. [1]
(c) Operating system. [1]
(d) (i) Any reasonable answer, for example: double click on the icon for the wordprocessing software. [1]
  (ii) Any reasonable answer, for example:
  – In the file menu, select Save As.
  – In the Save As dialogue box, set up the drive, directory and filename. [2]
  (iii) Any reasonable answer, for example:
  – The document will not be lost when the computer is switched off.
  – The document can be worked on using a compatible home computer. [2]

Total 12 marks

PRACTICE PAPER 2 – HIGHER LEVEL ANSWERS

Question 1
(a) 7 [1]
(b) 6 [1]
(c) (i) Any reasonable answer, for example: the Employee_Number 2342 is not unique. [1]
  (ii) Any Employee_Number that is not shown, for example, 1337. [1]

    (iii) Employee_Number.   [*1*]

    (iv) A key field is used to identify a record.   [*1*]

(d) Deleted; inserted; amended.   [*3*]

(e) (i)   Any reasonable answer, for example: an employee could receive too much pay.   [*1*]

    (ii)   Any reasonable answer, for example: Sex is M or Sex is F.   [*1*]

    (iii) Any reasonable answer, for example: give each employee a printed copy
         of the information stored and ask them if it is correct.   [*1*]

Total 12 marks

Question 2

(a) Any reasonable answer, for example: sum(B3:B9).   [*1*]

(b) Any reasonable answer, for example: text in A5; numbers in B3.   [*2*]

(c) C10, B11, B12 and B13.   [*1*]

(d) (i)   Any reasonable answer, for example:

        –   Once the spreadsheet has been set up, it is quicker for the contractor to use
            it than to work out all the calculations on a piece of paper.

        –   The contractor can be sure the calculations are carried out accurately.   [*2*]

    (ii)   Any reasonable answer, for example:

        –   The contractor must be able to use a computer and a spreadsheet.

        –   The contractor must have access to a computer and a spreadsheet.   [*2*]

(e) Any reasonable bar chart, for example:

   – Bar chart title is 'Mr Johnston's quote'.

   – Y axis is labelled 'cost of labour(£)' and has appropriate units.

   – X axis is labelled 'type of work' and shows these.

   – All the bars have the correct height.   [*4*]

Total 12 marks

Question 3

(a) (i)   A piece of software that appears to work like teletext to a user.   [*1*]

    (ii)   Any reasonable answer, for example: *Advantage*: customers can find
           information without taking up the time of TIC staff or when they are not
           available. *Disadvantage*: the TIC has to invest in the hardware and software
           needed to set up the system.   [*2*]

    (iii) Any reasonable answer, for example: *Advantage*: all the information is available
           to them in a form which they can easily search to find the accommodation
           they want. *Disadvantage*: they cannot take it away with them.   [*2*]

(b) These points, 1 mark each: teletext is cyclical and, as a result, slow to load some
     pages; fastext is the temporary storage of adjacent pages in RAM memory in the
     TV; fastext is only faster for pages in memory.   [*3*]

(c) Any reasonable answer, for example:

   –   The WWW is a GUI-based information service that runs on the Internet.

   –   You can access a wide range of information, for example, OFSTED reports
        and videos of important events happening in real time.   [*2*]

(d) Any reasonable answer, for example:

   –   Shopping is possible on the WWW because the user can pay on-line.

   –   Businesses with WWW sites can collect information about potential customers
        who access their sites.   [*2*]

Total 12 marks

Question 4

(a) Any reasonable answer, for example: there is a sensor in the road that detects the
     car as it approaches the traffic lights; the sensor is connected to the computer that
     controls the traffic lights.   [*2*]

(b) Any reasonable answer, for example:

   –   The control system runs different traffic management programs at different
        times of the day.

– The length of time the lights are on green is sensitive to the volume of traffic approaching the lights.
– The length of time the lights are on green is sensitive to other priorities, such as the need to make it easy for traffic to get out of city centres but hard to get into them.
– The length of time all lights are on red is longer to allow congestion on the junction to clear. [3]

(c) (i) Any reasonable answer, for example: connect every set of lights to the same control system; program the control system so that it changes the lights to green in front of traffic moving round the ring road at 30 mph. [2]

(ii) Any reasonable answer, for example: traffic police are not needed to catch drivers speeding as the control system encourages drivers to regulate their speed. [1]

(iii) Any reasonable answer, for example: the ring road is safer as there is advantage in considerate driving. [1]

(iv) Any reasonable answer, for example: less petrol is consumed when cars move at a steady speed, and this reduces emissions. [1]

(d) Any reasonable answer, for example:
– IT makes teleworking possible. This benefits the environment by reducing the need for workers to commute.
– Using e-mail reduces the need for paper, and the transport of mail by road, sea and air, thus helping to conserve resources. [2]

Total 12 marks

Question 5

(a) Any reasonable answer, for example: each product has a bar code on it; the bar code contains a product identification number that identifies the product; the bar code is input using a laser scanner; the check digit on the bar code is re-calculated to check validity; the product identification number is sent to the main computer; the product information file is searched to find a matching bar code; the price and description are sent to the checkout and printed on the receipt. [5]

(b) Any reasonable answer, for example: there is a re-order level on the product information file; the computer knows the actual stock level using this algorithm, actual stock = stock at start – sales + deliveries; if the actual stock is less than the re-order level, the supermarket's computer automatically connects to the supplier's computer and places an order. [3]

(c) Any reasonable answer, for example:
– The supermarket can monitor the quantity of goods handled by checkout assistants. This is a measure of how quickly they are working.
– The supermarket can have detailed information on when particular products sell well, and can place larger orders in anticipation of greater sales. [4]

Total 12 marks

LONGMAN
EXAM
PRACTICE
KITS

REVISION
PLANNER

No. of weeks before the exams	Date: Week commencing	MONDAY	TUESDAY
12			
11			
10			

WEDNESDAY	THURSDAY	FRIDAY	SATURDAY	SUNDAY

Get Revising   *Weeks 9 to 4*

Working on the basis of covering two topics per week an ideal pattern to follow for each week would be:

Read through your class notes and coursework.

Summarise the main points:

- write down the main principles/theories
- outline key terms and definitions
- note important examples/illustrations
- list important data/formula

(Using a highlighter pen is very useful here)

Practise answering exam questions:

- work through the questions in your Longman Exam Practice Kits
- write outline answers
- write full answers to some questions giving yourself the same time as in the exam
- make sure that you try to answer questions of each type set in the exam
- check your answers with those provided in your Longman Exam Practice Kit. Learn from any mistakes you have made.

Get Confidence   *Weeks 3 to 1*

- ➤ Have a final read through of all your class notes and coursework.
- ➤ Read through the summaries you have already made.
- ➤ Try to reduce these summary notes to a single side of A4 paper.
- ➤ Test yourself to check that you can remember everything on each A4 page.
- ➤ Go over the practice questions already attempted.

The day before the exams

- ➤ Read through each A4 summary sheet.
- ➤ Check that you have all the equipment you need for the exam.
- ➤ Do something you enjoy in the evening.
- ➤ Go to bed reasonably early: tired students rarely give their best.

The exam – get up and go

- ➤ Have a good breakfast to give you energy.
- ➤ Don't panic – everyone else is nervous too.
- ➤ Remember – the examiners are looking for opportunities to give you marks, not take them away!

Good luck!

No. of weeks before the exams	Date: Week commencing	MONDAY	TUESDAY
9			
8			
7			
6			
5			
4			
3			
2			
1			

Titles Available –

GCSE
Biology
Business Studies
Chemistry
English
French
Geography
German
Higher Maths
Information
Systems
Mathematics
Physics
Science

A-LEVEL
Biology
British and European
 Modern History
Business Studies
Chemistry
Economics
French
Geography
German
Mathematics
Physics
Psychology
Sociology

There are lots of ways to revise. It is important to find what works best for you. Here are some suggestions:

- try testing with a friend: testing each other can be fun!
- label or highlight sections of text and make a checklist of these items.
- learn to write summaries – these will be useful for revision later.
- try reading out loud to yourself.
- don't overdo it – the most effective continuous revision session is probably between forty and sixty minutes long.
- practise answering past exam papers and test yourself using the same amount of time as you will have on the actual day – this will help to make the exam itself less daunting.
- pace yourself, taking it step by step.

WEDNESDAY	THURSDAY	FRIDAY	SATURDAY	SUNDAY

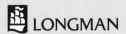